The Within Creates The Without

Daily Meditations

Creating Our Lives By Design

Complied By David Allen

A compilation from the archives of some of the best authors on how we create our lives by design

Metaphysics / Law of Attraction Edition

Copyright © 2019

Copyright © 2019 by David Allen / Shanon Allen

All rights reserved. No part of this publication may be reproduced, distributed, or transmitted in any form or by any means, including photocopying, recording, or other electronic or mechanical methods, without the prior written permission of the publisher, except in the case of brief quotations embodied in critical reviews and certain other noncommercial uses permitted by copyright law.
Printed in the United States of America

February 2019

ISBN: 978-0-9995435-7-3

Visit Us At **NevilleGoddardBooks.com** for a complete listing of all our books and **1000's of Free Books to Read online and download.**

Foreword

I feel these words by Robert Collier are very fitting as the foreword to this book.

Even now, with the limited knowledge at our command, we can control circumstances to the point of making the world without an expression of our own world within, where the real thoughts, the real power, resides. Through this world within you can find the solution of every problem, the cause for every effect. Discover it — and all power, all possession is within your control. For the world without is but a reflection of that world within. Your thought creates the conditions your mind images. Keep before your mind's eye the image of all you want to be and you will see it reflected in the world without. Think abundance, feel abundance, BELIEVE abundance, and you will find that as you think and feel and believe, abundance will manifest itself in your daily life. Your thoughts supply you with limitless energy which will take whatever form your mind demands. The thoughts are the mold which crystallizes this energy into good or ill according to the form you impress upon it. You are free to choose which. But whichever you choose, the result is sure. Thoughts of wealth, of power, of success, can bring only results commensurate with your idea of them. Thoughts of poverty and lack can bring only limitation and trouble.

Robert Collier

Acknowledgements

The Within Creates The Without: Daily Meditations is a compilation from the archives of the following authors

Charles F. Haanel, Charles Fillmore, Charles Wesley Kyle, Christian Larson, Emmett Fox, Ernest Holmes, Eugene Del Mar, Fay Adams, Floyd B Wilson, Genevieve Behrend, George Schubel, Helen Wilmans, Henry Thomas Hamblin, James Allen, Jeanie P. Owens, John Seaman Garns, Joseph Murphy, Leo Virgo, Mrs. Adam H. Dickey, Mrs. Evelyn Lowes Wicker, Orison Swett Marden, Prentice Mulford, R. C. Douglass, Robert Collier, Shirley Bell Hastings, Uriel Buchanan, Venice J. Bloodworth, Wallace Wattles, Walter C Lanyon, William Walker Atkinson

Contents

Legal	
Foreword	
Acknowledgements	
January	6
February	27
March	47
April	68
May	88
June	109
July	129
August	150
September	171
October	191
November	212
December	232
Metaphysical Books	252

January

The Within Creates The Without: Daily Meditations

January 1st

Joseph Murphy

I say to people who consult me regarding financial lack to "marry wealth." Some see the point; others do not. As all Bible students know, your wife is what you are mentally joined to, united with, or at one with. In other words, what you conceive and believe, you give conception. If you believe the world is cold, cruel, and harsh, that it is a "dog eat dog" way of life, that is your concept; you are married to it, and you will have children or issue by that marriage. The children from such a mental marriage or belief will be your experiences, conditions, and circumstances, together with all other events in your life. All your experiences and reactions to life will be the image and likeness of the ideas which fathered them. Look at the many wives the average man is living with, such as fear, doubt, anxiety, criticism, jealousy, and anger; these play havoc with his mind. Marry wealth by claiming, feeling, and believing: "God supplies all my needs according to his riches in glory." Or take the following statement, and repeat it over and over again knowingly until your consciousness is conditioned by it, or it becomes part of your meditation: "I AM Divinely expressed, and I have a wonderful income." Do not say this in a parrot-like fashion, but know that your train of thought is being engraved in your deeper mind, and it becomes a conditioned state of consciousness. Let the phrase become meaningful to you. Pour life, love, and feeling on it, making it alive.

January 2nd

James Allen

Thought and character are one, and as character can only manifest and discover itself through environment and circumstance, the outer conditions of a person's life will always be found to be harmoniously related to his inner state. This does not mean that a man's circumstances at any given time are an indication of his entire character, but that those circumstances are so intimately connected with some vital thought element within himself that, for the time being, they are indispensable to his development.

January 3rd

Robert Collier

Your body is for all practical purposes merely a machine which the mind uses. This mind is usually thought of as consciousness; but the conscious part of your mind is in fact the very smallest part of it. Ninety per cent of your mental life is subconscious, so when you make active use of only the conscious part of your mind you are using but a fraction of your real ability; you are running on low gear. And the reason why more people do not achieve success in life is because so many of them are content to run on low gear all their lives — on SURFACE ENERGY. If these same people would only throw into the fight the resistless force of their subconscious minds they would be, amazed at their undreamed of capacity for winning success.

January 4th

Ernest Holmes

Never struggle, Mind makes things out of Itself, there is no effort made. Don't think that there is so much to be overcome. Have only a calm sense of perfect peace as you realize that God is all, and that you are using the perfect law and that nothing can hinder it from working for you. Many people are learning to do this, and no one has yet failed to demonstrate who has been steadfast, using the law in a consistent and persistent trust. All that we have to do is to provide the right mental and spiritual attitude of mind and then believe that we already have, and the reward will be with us. We shall see it. The time will come when we will not have to demonstrate at all because we will be always living so near to the law that it will do all for us without much conscious thought on our part.

The Within Creates The Without: Daily Meditations

January 5th

Leo Virgo

The son of man, the I AM, is the door between mind formless and mind formed. "I AM the door; by me if any man enter in, he shall be saved, and shall go in and out, and find pasture," said Jesus. All things are from the One Mind, are the One Mind formed. But in its formed state the One Mind is as if it were separate from its formless self. Thus God gives Himself to His creations. He becomes subject to the will of His idea, man, on the plane of manifestation. This brings us to a point where we can see that every state of consciousness is mind manifest according to the intelligence recognized by the I AM. Thus every living thing is mind in its varying states of realization of infinite possibilities. The I AM in each of us is the door between the formless and the formed mind. We can look both ways, and draw sustenance from either side. If we look within for our supplies we are drawing direct from the Father, and "all power is given onto us in heaven and in earth." If we look without, and depend upon the external for our sustenance, we are limited to the conditions prevailing in that realm. Here is where judgment and discrimination should be exercised. He who has not reached a place where he can draw all his sustenance from the formless, and live alone on " every word that proceedeth out of the mouth of God," but is still bound to eating and drinking, should study the mental states of those things which he incorporates into his consciousness.

January 6th

Prentice Mulford

As regards your business, don't talk to anybody, man or woman, regarding your plans or projects, or anything connected with them, unless you are perfectly sure they wish for your success. Don't talk to people who hear you out of politeness. Every word so spoken represents so much force taken out of your project. The number you can talk to with profit is very small. But the good wish of one real friend, if he gives you a hearing but for ten minutes, is a literal, living, active force, added to your own, and from that time working in your behalf. If your aim is for right and justice you will be led to those you can trust and talk to with safety. Your spiritual being or sense will tell you whom you can trust. When you demand justice for yourself, you demand it for the whole race. If you allow yourself to be dominated, browbeaten, or cheated by others without inward or outward protest, you are condoning deceit and trickery. You are in league with it. Three persons engaged in any form of gossip, tattle, or scandal generate a force and send it from them of tattle, gossip, and scandal. The thought they send into the air returns to them and does them injury in mind and body. It is far more profitable to talk with others of things which go to work out good. Every sentence you speak is a spiritual force to you and others for good or ill.

January 7th

Christian Larson

Just be glad, and you always will be glad. You will have better reason to be glad. You will have more and more things to make you glad. For great is the power of sunshine, especially human sunshine. It can change anything, transform anything, remake anything, and cause anything to become as fair and beautiful as itself. Just be glad and your fate will change; a new life will begin and a new future will dawn for you. All things that are good and desirable will begin to come into your world in greater measure, and you will be enriched far beyond your expectations, both from the without and from the within. And the cause of the change is this, that all things respond to the call of rejoicing; all things gather where life is a song. When you are tempted to feel discouraged or disappointed, be glad instead. Know that you can, say that you will, and stand uncompromisingly upon your resolve. Be strong and be glad. For when strength and rejoicing combine in your soul, every trace of gloom or despair must disappear; because such conditions can exist only where weakness is the rule and mastery the exception. Combine strength with rejoicing and you will exercise a magic power and you will possess a secret that will serve you royally no matter what your difficulties or obstacles may be. All joy is light; and it is the light that dispels the darkness.

January 8th

George Schubel

Briefly stated, visualizing is an inner application of certain principles of which we can become cognizant by observing the corresponding outer application which we call photography. In fact, photography is visualizing made outwardly visible to our objective senses, it is visualizing visualized into outward form so that outward things can be reproduced for us in the same manner in which they a.re reproduced in the mind. Hence, if we begin our studies by an understanding of the theory and working processes of photography, we will begin to understand the theory and working processes involved in mental-photography, and at the same time we will lay the basis for an exact and definite science of visualizing which will serve us at all times and for every purpose. We know that when we apply the principles of photography; when we operate the mechanical parts of the camera — the lens, the range finder, the shutter, in a certain way; and when we apply the proper chemical elements in a proper manner, then we are able to reproduce an object with unerring accuracy. So with the mental-mechanical and chemical principles and faculties involved in reproducing our desires and thought-images. When we apply them correctly we will get outward results that are just as definite, just as truthful, just as accurate reproductions as those produced by the intelligent photographer.

January 9th

Ernest Holmes

What more can we ask! What greater realization of life than to know that God is with us! From this great realization comes peace, a peace which the world little understands, and a calm which is as deep as the infinite sea of love in which he realizes himself to be immersed. Peace brings poise, and the union of these two gives birth to Power. No person can hope to arrive while he believes in two powers; only as we rise to the realization of the One in and through all can we attain. When we speak the word there must be no confusion but only that calm reliance which knows that "Beside me there is none other." Realize that Spirit is All Causation, and that all things are made out of it, by the operation of the word through it, and that you can speak the word that is one with the Spirit and there will be no more confusion. "As the Father has inherent life in himself, so has he given to the Son to have inherent life within himself." "Speak the word only and it shall be done." "The word is in your own mouth that ye should know it and do it." "Stranger on earth, thy home is heaven; Pilgrim, thou art the guest of God."

January 10th

Leo Virgo

The son of man, the I AM, is the door between mind formless and mind formed. "I AM the door; by me if any man enter in, he shall be saved, and shall go in and out, and find pasture," said Jesus. All things are from the One Mind, are the One Mind formed. But in its formed state the One Mind is as if it were separate from its formless self. Thus God gives Himself to His creations. He becomes subject to the will of His idea, man, on the plane of manifestation. This brings us to a point where we can see that every state of consciousness is mind manifest according to the intelligence recognized by the I AM. Thus every living thing is mind in its varying states of realization of infinite possibilities. The I AM in each of us is the door between the formless and the formed mind. We can look both ways, and draw sustenance from either side. If we look within for our supplies we are drawing direct from the Father, and "all power is given onto us in heaven and in earth." If we look without, and depend upon the external for our sustenance, we are limited to the conditions prevailing in that realm. Here is where judgment and discrimination should be exercised. He who has not reached a place where he can draw all his sustenance from the formless, and live alone on " every word that proceedeth out of the mouth of God," but is still bound to eating and drinking, should study the mental states of those things which he incorporates into his consciousness.

January 11th

Fay Adams

When anyone reaches the state of mind where he is dissatisfied with things as they are and begins to look around for a happier solution of his problems, there comes the thought that if he was in a different place or some condition were removed, he could see a way out. The place to start is where you are, regardless of environment. The worse the condition the more imperative the start. The time is now, this minute. It is so easy to say, "As soon as I finish this task," or "Tomorrow I will be in a better frame of mind." Tomorrow you will probably feel worse and each day your DESIRE will grow less and the distressing conditions will fasten tighter on you, and sooner or later you will be as a useless bit of wreckage dashed about by each changing current of the life stream about you, struggling toward something today only to see it snatched away or to be knocked against some unseen obstacle the next or to be submerged by an overpowering sorrow at last. Goethe said, "A task once begun is half done,"

January 12th

Joseph Murphy

I am sure you have heard men say, "That fellow has a racket." "He is a racketeer." "He is getting money dishonestly." "He is a faker." "I knew him when he had nothing." "He is crooked, a thief, and a swindler." If you analyze the man who talks like that, he is usually in want or suffering from some financial or physical illness. Perhaps his former college friends went up the ladder of success and excelled him; now he is bitter and envious of their progress. In many instances this is the cause of his downfall. Thinking negatively of these classmates, and condemning their wealth, causes the wealth and prosperity he is praying for to vanish and flee away. He is condemning the things he is praying for.

He is praying two ways. On the one hand he is saying, "God is prospering me," and in the next breath, silently or audibly, he is saying, "I resent that fellow's wealth." Always make it a special point to bless the other person, and rejoice in his prosperity and success; when you do, you bless and prosper yourself.

January 13th

Christian Larson

What man is, and what man does, determines in what conditions, circumstances and environments he shall be placed. And since man can change both himself and his actions, he can determine what his fate is to be. To change himself, man must change his thought, because man is as he thinks; and to change his actions, he must change the purpose of his life, because every action is consciously or unconsciously inspired by the purpose held in view. To change his thought, man must be able to determine what impressions are to form in his mind, because every thought is created in the likeness of a mental impression. To choose his own mental impressions, man must learn to govern the objective senses, and must acquire the art of original thought. Everything that enters the mind through the physical senses will produce impressions upon the mind, unless prevented by original thought. These impressions will be direct reflections of the environment from whence they came; and since thoughts will be created in the exact likeness of these impressions, so long as man permits environment to impress the mind, his thoughts will be exactly like his environment: and since man becomes like the thoughts he thinks, he will also become like his environment. But man, in this way, not only grows into the likeness of his environment, but is, in addition, controlled by his environment, because his thoughts, desires, motives and actions are suggested to him by the impressions that he willingly accepts from environment. Therefore, one of the first essentials in the mastery of fate is to learn to govern the physical senses so thoroughly, that no impression can enter mind from without, unless it is consciously desired.

January 14th

Ernest Holmes

We trust our own word because first we "Know in whom we have believed." The sooner the one who is striving to attain will realize that truth must become revealed through his own soul, and not that of another, the sooner he will attain. We must then become immune from the race suggestion of an hypnotic power that sets itself up as an authority. There is no other authority than your own soul, as "There is no law but that your soul has set." Leave authorities to smaller minds, and to those who need a leader because of this their own self-confessed weakness, and be Free. Dare to "Stand amidst the eternal way" and proclaim your own Atonement with all the power that there is, was, or ever will be.

January 15th

Uriel Buchanan

Keep your mind in the thought of truth and purity, of health and vigor, and become as a magnet in the proper attitude of aspiration to attract the element of finer material. Every thought or desire to be better, more noble, more refined, every determination to rise above all that is selfish and sordid, arouses an element of strength which works in you and through you as a magnetic current of ever increasing power. You will gradually cut off the undesirable thought currents from inferior minds and will bring yourself in closer communication with the higher realm of thought and intelligence where all things needful will come to you. The mind should be trained persistently to shut out all morbid, depressing, fear currents of thought, and to be ever receptive to the positive, inspiring thought currents coming from helpful sources.

January 16th

Robert Collier

"It is one of the prominent doctrines of some of the oriental schools of practical psychology that the power of expelling thoughts, or if need be, killing them dead on the spot, must be attained. Naturally the art requires practice, but like other arts, when once acquired there is no mystery or difficulty about it. It is worth practice. It may be fairly said that life only begins when this art has been acquired. For obviously when, instead of being ruled by individual thoughts, the whole flock of them in their immense multitude and variety and capacity is ours to direct and dispatch and employ where we list, life becomes a thing so vast and grand, compared to what it was before, that its former condition may well appear almost ante-natal. If you can kill a thought dead, for the time being, you can do anything else with it that you please. And therefore it is that this power is so valuable. And it not only frees a man from mental torment (which is nine-tenths at least of the torment of life), but it gives him a concentrated power of handling mental work absolutely unknown to him before. The two are correlative to each other."

January 17th

James Allen

Law, not confusion, is the dominating principle in the universe. Justice, not injustice, is the soul and substance of life. And righteousness, not corruption, is the molding and moving force in the spiritual government of the world. This being so, man has but to right himself to find that the universe is right; and during the process of putting himself right, he will find that as he alters his thoughts toward things and other people, things and other people will alter toward him. The proof of this truth is in every person, and it therefore admits of easy investigation by systematic introspection and self-analysis. Let a man radically alter his thoughts, and he will be astonished at the rapid transformation it will effect in the material conditions of his life.

January 18th

Venice J. Bloodworth

Thoughts Are Things. Thought causes vibration and sets in motion the Law of Mind. Since everything has its beginning in mind, and as thought, which is mind in action, produces form, we realize that thought is creative. That which we call our subconscious mind, being a point in Universal Creative Law and being immediately available to us, guarantees that we have at our disposal the use of a law which is not only immediate, being inside of us, but it is also in connection with everything else in the universe. It is the belief in separation from God which keeps our good away from us. It is the belief that binds us, and not any actual power. We are really bound by our false beliefs, and we shall never be permanently free until we experience a complete change of thought. This is what is meant by "The Renewing of the Mind."

January 19th

Ernest Holmes

If the word is the way that God creates, it is the right way. If it works for God, shall it not work for us? As yet our word is more or less imperfect; but more and more it will become perfect, and so the outer condition will be brought up to the inner word. All words have as much power as we put into them when we speak. "The word is already in our own mouths." That word is all that you will ever need to bring happiness, health and success to you. Do you wish to live in a perfect world peopled with friends who love you, surrounded by all that is beautiful and pleasing? Do you wish to have the good things of life? There is but one way and that way is as sure as that the sun shines. Forget all else and think only upon what you want. Control all thought that denies the real, and as the mist disappears before the sun so shall all adversity melt before the shining radiance of your own exalted thought.

January 20th

Christian Larson

Whenever you see a man or woman who is different, who seems to stand out distinct, and who has something vital about them that no one else seems to possess, you have someone whose individuality is highly developed, and you also have someone who is going to make their mark in the world. Take two people of equal power, ability and efficiency, but with this difference. In the one individuality is highly developed, while in the other it is not. You know at once which one of these two is going to reach the highest places in the world of achievement; and the reason is that the one who possesses individuality lives above mind and body, thereby being able to control and direct the forces and powers of mind and body. The man or woman, however, whose individuality is weak, lives more or less down in mind and body, and instead of controlling mind and body, is constantly being influenced by everything from the outside that may enter their consciousness. Whenever you find a man or a woman who is doing something worthwhile, who is creating an impression upon the race, who is moving forward towards greater and better things, you find the individuality strong, positive and highly developed. It is therefore absolutely necessary that you give your best attention to the development of a strong, positive individuality if you wish to succeed in the world and make the best use of the forces in your possession. A negative or weak individuality drifts with the stream of environment, and usually receives only what others choose to give, but a firm, strong, positive, well-developed individuality, actually controls the ship of their life and destiny, and sooner or later will gain possession of what they originally set out to secure. A positive individuality has the power to take hold of things and turn them to good account. This is one reason why such an individuality always succeeds. Another reason is that the more fully your individuality is developed, the more you are admired by everybody with whom you may come in contact. The human race loves power, and counts it a privilege to give lofty positions to those who have power, and every man or woman whose individuality is highly developed, does possess power — usually exceptional power.

January 21st

Joseph Murphy

We must not let fear step in; for it is the opposite of love. Fear is the inversion of love, or love turned upside down. There is only Love. If a man recognizes love in a dog, the animal responds in kind. When we fear the dog or any other animal, the latter senses it, and strikes up a similar response in him. When we are faced with a problem, let us become still; feel within ourselves that Divine Love is working through the situation now; realize only harmony and peace prevail; then dismiss it from our minds knowing that it is so. We will find a perfect solution is offered to us which blesses all.

January 22nd

Jeanie P. Owens

The power that our thoughts have in affecting the conditions, all the conditions of our lives, is almost incredible to those who have paid no attention to the subject. It is no new discovery, although it is only of late that people seem to be waking up to its real importance. The statement in Proverbs, "As a man thinketh in his heart, so is he, "puts in a nutshell what might take whole volumes to explain fully. "As a man thinketh;" the one thing that we must all do at all times is to think; our minds are incessantly working whether we are conscious of it or not, and when we learn that each thought, however apparently trivial, has an actual value in shaping our character, we can readily understand what a mighty force for good or ill we hold within us. It is the method by which we work out our own salvation, for we must remember that in all God does, He works according to law, and this power of thought is one of the greatest spiritual laws yet known to us. " What we think we become." We have the divine gift of free-will, and the shaping of our lives lies to a very large extent in our own hands; we can make or mar them as we will.

January 23rd

Floyd B. Wilson

As years go by and students in the West are learning of the powers that may be awakened by silence, the possibilities of man are becoming more apparent, until all intelligence is now declaring that limitations to him are inconceivable. Little by little men are learning in the West that silence, which is the hall of learning to the Hindu, is indeed the hall of learning to all mankind. The great question with which, the undisciplined are wrestling is how to find the silence, when and how to come to it, and more than all, how to enter it in faith. I will not attempt in this paper to present any argument as to why the silence can properly be called the hall of learning, or why the greatest unfoldment the human can ever know must be developed in the silence. I assume that this is conceded, and come forward with the broad statement that to silence man must come in order that he may unfold the higher consciousness within him. Assuming this statement to be true, and assuring my readers that I have proved it true over and over again, both in my own investigations, and by comparison with others who have followed similar lines of work, I now come to the real purpose of this paper, which is to suggest how to go into the silence and permit the Universal to act in order that unfoldment which will fill the heart's desire may follow.

January 24th

Ernest Holmes

Man does not really create. He uses creative power that already is. Relatively speaking, he is the creative power in his own life; and so far as his thought goes, there is something that goes with it that has the power to bring forth into manifestation the thing thought of. Hitherto men have used this creative power in ignorance and so have brought upon themselves all kinds of conditions, but today hundreds of thousands are beginning to use these great laws of their being in a conscious, constructive way. Herein lies the great secret of the New Thought movements under their various names and cults and orders. All are using the same law even though some deny to others the real revelation. We should get into an attitude of mind wherein we should recognize the truth wherever we may find it.

January 25th

Charles F. Haanel

Harmony in the world within will be reflected in the world without by harmonious conditions, agreeable surroundings, the best of everything. It is the foundation of health and a necessary essential to all greatness, all power, all attainment, all achievement and all success. Harmony in the world within means the ability to control our thoughts, and to determine for ourselves how any experience is to affect us. Harmony in the world within results in optimism and affluence; affluence within results in affluence without. The world without reflects the circumstances and the conditions of the consciousness within. If we find wisdom in the world within, we shall have the understanding to discern the marvelous possibilities that are latent in this world within, and we shall be given the power to make these possibilities manifest in the world without. As we become conscious of the wisdom in the world within, we mentally take possession of this wisdom, and by taking mental possession we come into actual possession of the power and wisdom necessary to bring into manifestation the essentials necessary for our most complete and harmonious development. The world within is the practical world in which the men and women of power generate courage, hope, enthusiasm, confidence, trust and faith, by which they are given the fine intelligence to see the vision and the practical skill to make the vision real. Life is an unfoldment, not accretion. What comes to us in the world without is what we already possess in the world within. All possession is based on consciousness. All gain is the result of an accumulative consciousness. All loss is the result of a scattering consciousness.

January 26th

Christian Larson

We know that we can accomplish anything when we have sufficient power; and we also know that, in the creative life of the mind, there is sufficient power for anything we may desire to achieve or realize. It is only a matter of calling it forth into definite and tremendous action; and this, a brilliant imagination or a dazzling vision can do; provided, of course, that such a vision is maintained until the miracle is wrought. This proves what a priceless advantage we possess when we have an imagination that is not only brilliant, but so well trained that it will work exactly as we say. And methods are now available through which imagination and visioning power may be developed and trained to the greatest and most perfect degree. The creative power of the mind will work continuously and effectively for that which we think of the most. If we think the most of the commonplace, then the commonplace will be produced for us — in our minds, in our work, in our personal experience, in every way. But if we think the most of the good, the beautiful, the great and the wonderful — the creative power within will work and produce accordingly. And so true and exact is this aspect of the law, that any individual can determine what he is to become, and what his future is to be, by deciding specifically what he is to think of the most. Here we meet a remarkable subject; and the leading question will be what we should think of the most, so as to secure the results we desire. What we are to think of the most is determined largely by the purpose we have in life; by the pleasures we enjoy; by our desires and ambitions; by our ideals and aspirations; by our environment and associations; by our fears and worries; and by that which we admire, love and worship. It is imperative, therefore, that we purpose to make the most of life; that we seek only great pleasures; that we train ourselves to desire the purest, the greatest and the highest in every direction; that our ambitions be powerful and superior; that our ideals and aspirations be the most lofty and the most perfect we can possibly vision; that we improve and refine our environment, and associate only with the very best; that we fear not at all, nor worry; that our outlook be vast, and our visions high; that we love and admire the good, the true, the beautiful, the superior, the perfect — and with our deepest devotion; that we worship the highest conceivable, and look up to the infinitely great. To state the matter in brief: the creative power of the mind — the greatest power we possess — will work for that which we keep in mind; and the best way to keep in mind, or place in mind, what we want this power to produce and create for us, is to make extensive and intelligent use of purpose and expectation, determination and desire, vision and imagination, and related factors. To secure the best results, we should write out a program of great expectations, great desires, great visions, and so on; a program that would specify what we are determined to have; what we believe in tremendously; what we positively purpose to achieve, realize and become; and what we want the future to be. We should concentrate upon this program for a few moments every day — deeply knowing that the wonder power within is working continuously to bring it all to pass.

January 27th

Genevieve Behrend

Some persons feel that it is not quite proper to visualize for things. "It's too material," they say. Why, material form is necessary for the self-recognition of Spirit from the individual standpoint, and this is the means through which the Creative Process is carried forward. Therefore, far from matter being an illusion and something which ought not to be, matter is the necessary channel for the self-differentiation of Spirit. However, it is not my desire to lead you into lengthy and tiresome scientific reasoning, in order to remove the mystery from visualization and to put it upon a logical foundation. Naturally, each individual will do this in his own way. My only wish is to point out to you the easiest way I know, which is the road on which Troward guides me. I feel sure you will conclude, as I have, that the only mystery in connection with visualizing is the mystery of life taking form, governed by unchangeable and easily understood laws. We all possess more power and greater possibilities than we realize, and visualizing is one of the greatest of these powers, it brings other Possibilities to our observation. When we pause to think for a moment, we realize that for a cosmos to exist at all, it must be the outcome of a Cosmic Mind, which binds "all individual minds to a certain generic unity of action, thereby producing all things as realities and nothing as illusions."

January 28th

Henry Thomas Hamblin

The subconscious mind can be made to do more and more work for us if we will delegate definite work for it to deal with. One who has learnt thought control, who can take up a matter, consider it in all its bearings, and then dismiss the subject from his conscious thought, is able to increase his efficiency a hundred percent, and reduce his mental fatigue almost to vanishing point. Instead of laboriously working out his problems and worrying and scheming over them, he simply dismisses them to his subconscious mind to be dealt with by a master mind which works unceasingly, with great rapidity, extreme accuracy and entirely without effort. It is necessary, however, to give the subconscious every available information, for it possesses no inspiration or super-human wisdom, but works out logically, according to the facts supplied to it. This great, natural, untiring 'mind downstairs,' as it has been called, is also capable of doing even more useful work still. A writer or speaker or preacher can collect notes and ideas for his article, book, speech or sermon, and pass them down to his subconscious mind with orders that they be arranged in suitable order, division, sub-division and so on. When he comes either to write or prepare the notes of his speech or sermon, he will find all the work done for him, and all that he has to do is to write it down, entirely without effort or fatigue.

January 29th

Ernest Holmes

As law works without variation, so does the law of attraction work the same way. All that we have to do is to drop the undesired thing from our thought, forgive ourselves and start anew. We must never even think of it again. Let go of it once and for all. Our various experiences will teach us more and more to try to mold all of our thoughts and desires, so that they will be in line with the fundamental purpose of the Great Mind, the expression of that which is perfect. To fear to make conscious use of the Law would be to paralyze all efforts of progress. More and more will we come to see that a great cosmic plan is being worked out, and that all we have to do is to lend ourselves to it, in order that we may attain unto a real degree of life. As we do subject our thought to the greater purposes we are correspondingly blest, because we are working more in line with the Father, who from the beginning knew the end. We should never lose sight of the fact that we are each given the individual right to use the law, and that we cannot escape from using it.

January 30th

Prentice Mulford

Ten minutes spent in growling at your luck, or in growling at others because they have more luck than yourself, means ten minutes of your own force spent in making worse your own health and fortune. Every thought of envy or hatred sent another is a boomerang. It flies back to you and hurts you. The envy or dislike we may feel toward those who, as some express it, " put on airs," the ugly feeling we may have at seeing others riding in carriages and "rolling in wealth,' represents just so much thought (i. e. force) most extravagantly expended, for in its expenditure we get not only unhappiness but destroy future fortune and happiness. If this has been your common habit or mood of mind, do not expect to get out of it at once. Once you are convinced of the harm done you by such mood, a new force has come to gradually remove the old mind and bring a new one. But all changes must be gradual. Your own private room is your chief workshop for generating your spiritual force and building yourself up. If it is kept in disorder, if things are flung recklessly about, and you cannot lay your hands instantly upon them, it is an indication that your mind is in the same condition, and therefore your mind as it works on others, in carrying out your projects, will work with less effect and result by reason of its disordered and disorganized condition.

January 31st

Orison Swett Marden

The law cannot pity or help you if you break a bone, or are injured, any more than the law of electricity can help you when you abuse it. It will kill you if you break the law. To think about and worry about the things we do not want, or to fear that they will come to us, is but to invite them; because every impression becomes an expression, or tends to become so unless the impression is neutralized by its opposite. If we think too much about our losses, too much about our possible failure, all these things will tend to bring to us the very thing we are trying to get away from. On every hand we see this law of like attracting like exemplified in the lives of the poverty-stricken multitudes, who, through ignorance of the law, keep themselves in their unfortunate condition by saturating their minds with the poverty idea; thinking and acting and talking poverty; living in the belief in its permanency; fearing, dreading, and worrying about it. They do not realize, no one has ever told them, that as long as people mentally see the hunger wolf at the door and the poorhouse ahead of them; as long as they expect nothing but lack and poverty and hard conditions, they are headed toward these things; they are making it impossible for prosperity to come in their direction. The way to attract prosperity and drive poverty out of the life is to work in harmony with the law instead of against it. To expect prosperity, to believe with all your heart, no matter how present conditions may seem to contradict, that you are going to become prosperous, that you are already so, is the very first condition of the law of attaining what you desire. You cannot get it by doubting or fearing. Whatever we visualize and work for we will get.

February

February 1st

Christian Larson

A number of people have a habit of saying, "Something is always wrong"; but why should we not say instead, "Something is always right"? We would thereby express more of the truth and give our minds a more wholesome tendency. It is not true that something is always wrong. When we compare the wrong with the right, the wrong is always in the minority. However, it is the effect of such thinking upon the mind that we wish to avoid, whether the wrong be in our midst or not. When you think that there is always something wrong, your mind is more or less concentrated on the wrong, and will therefore create the wrong in your own mentality; but when you train yourself to think there is always something right, your mind will concentrate upon the right, and accordingly will create the right. And when the mind is trained to create the right it will not only produce right conditions within itself, but all thinking will tend to become right; and right thinking invariably leads to health, happiness, power and plenty. The average person is in the habit of saying, "The older I get"; and they thereby call the attention of the mind to the idea that they are getting older. In brief, they compel their mind to believe that they are getting older and older, and thereby direct the mind to produce more and more age. The true expression in this connection is, "The longer I live." This expression calls the mind's attention to the length of life, which will, in turn, tend to increase the power of that process in you that can prolong life. When people reach the age of sixty or seventy, they usually speak of "the rest of my days," thus implying the idea that there are only a few more days remaining. The mind is thereby directed to finish life in a short period of time, and accordingly, all the forces of the mind will proceed to work for the speedy termination of personal existence. The correct expression is "from now on," as that leads thought into the future indefinitely without impressing the mind with any end whatever.

February 2nd

Ernest Holmes

In metaphysics, as in everything else, if we want to accomplish results, we have got to do something with our principle. It is not enough to say all is Spirit and all is Mind. That won't heal you. It is not enough to say God is good. That will never do it. God is good; that might be a part of it. Everything in the universe is good, but if we are actually to change our conditions and heal our bodies, we have to take the principle of life and scientifically apply it. It is not enough for you and me to sit down and say electricity is and electricity is wonderful and it is illuminating. Unless we take the principle of electricity and apply it for a definite purpose, it will not illuminate anything. The reason more people do not succeed in metaphysics in the way of demonstrating is that they do not realize that Mind has to be applied. They think they can sit down and say God is good and God is all and that will do it. Now, it won't do it, and the people who do not do more than that do not get results. The people who get results realize the mental principle, realize they get results in the universe through mental law and that they govern in their own life through mental law and they begin to use that mental law of causation, creative power, and allow it to flow through them. They begin definitely to use it as a great law of attraction setting up within their own consciousness a center for a definite purpose and realizing that toward that center there will gravitate the thing they desire; realizing there is a power behind it which is intelligent, which makes it operate, which relieves them of personal responsibility so that all the individual has to do is to know within. And that person who can know the most definitely and the most clearly and at the same time with the greatest sense of ease and peace, devoid of all fear, being absolutely sure, that is the person who will make the best demonstration.

February 3rd

Joseph Murphy

You can bring into your life more power, more wealth, more health, more happiness, and more joy by learning to contact and release the hidden power of your subconscious mind. You need not acquire this power; you already possess it. But, you want to learn how to use it; you want to understand it so that you can apply it in all departments of your life. Through the wisdom of your subconscious mind you can attract the ideal companion, as well as the right business associate or partner. It can find the right buyer for your home, and provide you with all the money you need, and the financial freedom to be, to do, and to go, as your heart desires. It is your right to discover this inner world of thought, feeling, and power, of light, love, and beauty. Though invisible, its forces are mighty. Within your subconscious mind you will find the solution for every problem, and the cause for every effect. Because you can draw out the hidden powers, you come into actual possession of the power and wisdom necessary to move forward in abundance, security, joy, and dominion.

February 4th

Floyd B. Wilson

Since man has made a study of his mental powers he has found it necessary when troubled or annoyed to go where he could be alone, and there, as he has termed it, gather himself together again. Long before the metaphysics of today came into prominence, man had learned when exhausted and worried, that his best way to recuperate was to be alone. It was not a question of doing quiet thinking; it perhaps was not a question of thinking at all; and yet from these lonely musings he came forth renewed in strength and courage, ready again to battle with the world. With the Hindu, meditation is the path to power. He has studied unfoldment, as men in the West, with the hurry and rush of business, never thought of doing.

February 5th

James Allen

Each man is circumscribed by his own thoughts, but he can gradually extend their circle; he can enlarge and elevate his mental sphere. He can leave the low, and reach up to the high; he can refrain from harboring thoughts that are dark and hateful, and can cherish thoughts that are bright and beautiful; and as he does his, he will pass into a higher sphere of power and beauty, will become conscious of a more complete and perfect world. For men live in spheres low or high according to the nature of their thoughts. Their world is as dark and narrow as they conceive it to be, as expansive and glorious as their comprehensive capacity. Everything around them is tinged with the color of their thoughts.

February 6th

Robert Collier

What is true of the principle of mathematics is true of every principle. The principle is changeless, undying. It is only our expression of the principle that changes as our understanding of it becomes more thorough. Lightning held only terror for man until he made of electricity his servant. Steam was only so much waste until man learned to harness it. Fire and water are the most destructive forces known — until properly used, then they are man's greatest helpers. There is nothing wrong with any gift of God — once we find the way to use it. The truth is always there if we can find the principle behind it. The figures in mathematics are never bad. It is merely our incorrect arrangement of them. The great need is an open mind and the desire for understanding. How far in the science of mathematics would you get if you approached the study of it with the preconceived notion that two plus two makes five, and nothing you heard to the contrary was going to change that belief? "Except ye turn, and become as little children, ye shall not enter into the kingdom of heaven." You must drop all your preconceived ideas, all your prejudices. You must never say — "Oh, that sounds like so-and-so. I don't want any of it." Just remember that any great movement must have at least a grain of truth back of it, else it could never grow to any size. Seek that grain of truth.

February 7th

Ernest Holmes

Always remember this. Life is from within outward, and never from without inward. You are the center of power in your own life. Be sure and not take on false suggestion. The world is full of calamity howlers; turn from them, every one, no matter how great you think they may be; you haven't the time to waste over anything that is negative. You are a success, and you are giving to the Law, every day, just what you want done. And the Law is always working for you. All fear has gone and you know that there is but One Power in all the Universe. Happy is the man who knows this, the greatest of all Truths. The whole thing resolves itself into our mental ability to control our thought. The man who can do this, can have what he wants, can do what he wishes, and becomes what he wills. Life, God, the Universe, is his.

February 8th

Christian Larson

When we proceed to train the subconscious along any line, or for special results, we must always comply with the following law: The subconscious responds to the impressions, the suggestions, the desires, the expectations and the directions of the conscious mind, provided that the conscious touches the subconscious at the time. The secret therefore is found in the two phases of the mind touching each other as directions are being made; and to cause the conscious to touch the subconscious, it is necessary to feel conscious action penetrating your entire interior system; that is, you should feel at the time that you are living not simply on the surface, but through and through. At such times, the mind should be calm and in perfect poise, and should be conscious of that finer, greater something within you that has greater depth than mere surface existence. When you wish to direct the subconscious to produce physical health, first picture in your mind a clear idea of perfect health. Try to see this idea with the mind's eye, and then try to feel the meaning of this idea with consciousness, and while you are in the attitude of that feeling, permit your thought and your attention to pass into that deep quiet, serene state of being wherein you can feel the mental idea of wholeness and health entering into the very life of every atom in your system. In brief, try to feel perfectly healthy in your mind and then let that feeling sink into your entire physical system. Whenever you feel illness coming on, you can nip it in the bud by this simple method, because if the subconscious is directed to produce more health, added forces of health will soon begin to come forth from within, and put out of the way, so to speak, any disorder or ailment that may be on the verge of getting a foothold in the body.

February 9th

Venice J. Bloodworth

God created us, but we make ourselves. We are the architects and builders of our own destiny. Our lives contain no joy that was not born in our imagination, and crystallized into outward expression by the power of our own thoughts. Sorrow, sickness and failure spring from fear, and negative thinking, and are self-imposed — always. We fear poverty, sickness, hard-luck, accidents and disaster. We all have our own special brand of fear, and what foundation have these fear thoughts? NONE! They come from false appearance, heredity, environment, race consciousness, and not one is born of right thinking. They are the appearance of evil. How are these negative thoughts to be overcome? Not by opposition, for opposition to evil implies its reality, and evil of itself never was and never can be real. We count as evil that which does not bring good results, and the word "sin" is attached to those acts which bring discord and unhappiness. Evil and sin are not causes, but results; and cannot be placed among principles. All principles are good. It is only when we fail to use principles correctly that we sin or fall short. "Fallen Short" is the original meaning of the Greek word from which our word "Sin" is derived.

February 10th

Helen Wilmans

Self-generated thought is the vital fluid itself. It courses through a man's veins, and stimulates him to undreamed activities. But he needs to draw it fresh from the fountain-head of his own organism each day. Therefore, he must at once turn his back on the beliefs of the present age — on all of them — for they are not his. Even those among them which are truest are not properly related to him by the divine parentage of his own creative functions; and so he must let them go, and step clear from them all in absolute nakedness. He must then search his own organism for the well-spring of original thought, and bring it forth in which to clothe himself. For man is a mental being, and truth, in a thousand forms, is the Life Principle lying latent and made visible by his own recognition of it. This is the true method of mental growth — which is also "physical" growth — for as sure as the world turns on its axis, Walt Whitman was right when he said: "The soul is the body and the body is the soul." For a man is whole. His so-called physical being is his mental being, and the ever progressive unfoldment of the mental will be the ever progressive unfoldment of the physical.

February 11th

Wallace Wattles

There is an invincible power in you, and the same power is in the things you want. It is bringing them to you and bringing you to them. This is a thought that you must grasp, and hold continuously that the same intelligence that is in you is in the things you desire. They are impelled toward you as strongly and decidedly as your desire impels you toward them. The tendency, therefore, of a steadily held thought must be to bring the things you desire to you and to group them around you. So long as you hold your thought and your faith right all must go well. Nothing can be wrong but your own personal attitude, and that will not be wrong if you trust and are not afraid. Hurry is a manifestation of fear; he who fears not has plenty of time. If you act with perfect faith in your own perceptions of truth, you will never be too late or too early; and nothing will go wrong. If things appear to be going wrong, do not get disturbed in mind; it is only in appearance. Nothing can go wrong in this world but yourself; and you can go wrong only by getting into the wrong mental attitude.

February 12th

Ernest Holmes

The atmosphere created by a real lover of the race is so powerful that although his other shortcomings may be many, still the world will love him in return. "To him who loveth much, much will be forgiven." People are dying for real human interest, for someone to tell them that they are all right. Which person do we like the better: the one who is always full of trouble and faultfinding, or the one who looks at the world as his friend and loves it? The question does not need to be asked; we know that we want the company of the person who loves and loving, forgets all else. The only reason we think other people are "queer" is because they do not happen to think as we do. We must get over this little, petty attitude and see things in the large. The person who sees what he wants to see, regardless of what appears, will someday experience in the outer what he has so faithfully seen within.

February 13th

Uriel Buchanan

Imagination is the eye of the mind. It should be trained to image only the highest. A disordered imagination will confuse the mind and dissipate the energies. But when controlled by the will you can direct it to see yourself in better environments. And the more you do this in imagination, the greater will be your power to make the picture a reality. Live over in mind the acts you should perform, the words you should utter and the attitude you should assume to take hold of the world and win from it the things you demand. Was not the world made for you? Who has a greater right than you to enjoy the beauties of nature and art, to have the glow and symmetry of health, and to possess the treasures which the earth contains and the sea hides? The world is your estate. It is yours by the divine right of universal humanity. Recognizing this fact, train your imagination to see yourself surrounded by every luxury. See yourself with others who are bright and prosperous. Imagine that you are courageous, that you are gifted, that you have tact and that you have irresistible power. The things you hold most in thought and imagination you will make a reality. But there must be steadfastness of purpose and persistent faith and effort. To say to yourself daily, "I can and I will," to send an unbroken current of thought in the direction of the desire, to aim well and to neglect nothing that will aid you, will insure the final realization of every reasonable ambition. But if you have courage today and make spasmodic efforts, and the next day feel depressed and are doubtful, you will send out destructive forces which will hinder your progress. Negative, despondent, irritable thoughts are as potent to destroy as are positive, hopeful, courageous thoughts to build up. If your mind wanders, if you doubt and hesitate, if you lack faith and persistency of purpose, you will continue to drift with the tide of circumstances discouraged and helpless on life's surging sea.

February 14th

Christian Larson

To develop individuality, the first essential is to give the "I AM" its true and lofty position in your mind. The "I AM" is the very centre of individuality, and the more fully conscious you become of the "I AM" the more of the power that is in the "I AM" you arouse, and it is the arousing of this power that makes individuality positive and strong. Another essential is to practice the idea of feeling or conceiving yourself as occupying the masterful attitude. Whenever you think of yourself, think of yourself as being and living and acting in the masterful attitude. Then in addition, make every desire positive, make every feeling positive, make every thought positive, and make every action of mind positive. To make your wants distinct and positive, that is, to actually and fully know what you want and then proceed to want what you want with all the power that is in you, will also tend to give strength and positiveness to your individuality; and the reason is that such actions of mind will tend to place in positive, constructive action every force that is in your system. A most valuable method is to picture in your mind your own best idea of what a strong, well-developed individuality would necessarily be, and then think of yourself as becoming more and more like that picture. In this connection it is well to remember that we gradually grow into the likeness of that which we think of the most. Therefore, if you have a very clear idea of a highly developed individuality, and think a great deal of that individuality with a strong, positive desire to develop such an individuality, you will gradually and surely move towards that lofty ideal. Another valuable method is to give conscious recognition to what may be called the bigger man on the inside. Few people think of this greater man that is within them, but we cannot afford to neglect this interior entity for a moment. This greater or larger man is not something that is separate and distinct from ourselves. It is simply the sum-total of the greater powers and possibilities that are within us. We should recognize these, think of them a great deal, and desire with all the power of heart and mind and soul to arouse and express more and more of these inner powers.

February 15th

Prentice Mulford

When we come really to love God or the Infinite Spirit of Good, we shall love every part of God. A tree is a part of God. When we come to send out our love to it, it will send its love back, and that love–that literal mind and element coming from the tree to us will enter our beings, add itself to them and give us its knowledge and power. It will tell us that the mind and force it represents of the Infinite has far better uses for man than to be turned into fuel or lumber. Their love will tell us that the forests piercing the air as they do with their billions of branches, twigs and leaves, are literal conductors for a literal element which they bring to the earth. This element is life giving to man, in proportion to his capacity for receiving it. The nearer we are to a conception of the Infinite Mind–the clearer is it seen by us that this mind pervades all things–the closer we feel our relationship to the tree, bird or animal as a fellow creature, the more can we absorb of the vitalizing element given out by all these expressions of mind. The person who looks on trees as fit only for fuel and lumber, can get but little of this element, which to the finer mind is an elixir of life. The mind which sees in tree, bird, animal, fish or insect only a thing lacking intelligence and fit only to destroy or enslave for amusement, repels from all of these a spirit or element, which, if recognized, would be received or absorbed, and, if absorbed, would bring a new life and power to mind and body. We get the element of love only in proportion as we have it in us. We can only draw this element from the Supreme Power. We draw it in proportion as we admire every expression of the Infinite, be that expression tree, or shrub, or insect, or bird, or other form of the Natural, We cannot destroy or mutilate what we really love. The more of these things we really love, the more of their element of love flows to us. That element is for us life as real Is the tree itself. The more of that life we are receiving and absorbing, the more shall we realize a power in life, which can only be expressed as miraculous.

February 16th

Genevieve Behrend

It should be steadily borne in mind that there is an Intelligence and Power in all Nature and all space, which is always creative and infinitely sensitive and responsive. The responsiveness of its nature is two-fold: it is creative, and amenable to suggestion. Once the human understanding grasps this all-important fact, it realizes the simplicity with which the law of life supplies your every demand. All that is necessary is to realize that your mind is a center of Divine operation, and consequently contains that within itself which accepts suggestions, and expect all life to respond to your call. Then you will find suggestions which tend to the fulfillment of your desire coming to you, not only from your fellowmen, but also from the flowers, the grass, the trees, and the rocks, which will enable you to fulfill your heart's desire, if you act upon them in confidence on this physical plane. "Faith without works is dead," but Faith with Works sets you absolutely free.

February 17th

Ernest Holmes

Principle itself is simplicity, yet it is infinite . . it is Infinite Mind and manifestation of Mind. We live in a Spiritual universe governed through thought, or the word which first becomes law; this law creates what we call matter. Jesus Christ discerned the truth about spiritual principles more than any other man who ever lived, and he proclaimed the eternal reign of law and understanding, absolute, complete, perfect; and he found that law to be operative through his own thought and the power of his own word. And when you and I shall cease looking outside ourselves to any person and shall realize that whatever truth and whatever power we shall have must flow through us; when we begin to interpret our own natures, we shall begin to understand God and law, and life, and not until then.

February 18th

Joseph Murphy

The principle reasons for failure are: Lack of confidence and too much effort. Many people block answers to their prayers by failing to fully comprehend the workings of their subconscious mind. When you know how your mind functions, you gain a measure of confidence. You must remember whenever your subconscious mind accepts an idea; it immediately begins to execute it. It uses all its mighty resources to that end and mobilizes all the mental and spiritual laws of your deeper mind. This law is true for good or bad ideas. Consequently, if you use it negatively, it brings trouble, failure, and confusion. When you use it constructively, it brings guidance, freedom, and peace of mind.

February 19th

James Allen

Let a man cease from his sinful thoughts, and all the world will soften toward him, and be ready to help him. Let him put away his weakly and sickly thoughts, and lo! opportunities will spring up on every hand to aid his strong resolves. Let him encourage good thoughts, and no hard fate shall bind him down to wretchedness and shame. The world is your kaleidoscope, and the varying combinations of colors which at every succeeding moment it presents to you are the exquisitely adjusted pictures of your ever moving thoughts.

February 20th

Christian Larson

The creative energies of mind are constantly producing thought, and these thoughts will be produced in the likeness of the deepest, the clearest and the most predominant mental impressions. Therefore, it is absolutely necessary that the predominant impressions be those into the likeness of which we desire to grow, because, as the impressions are, so are the thoughts; and as the thoughts are, so is man. When man thinks that he will succeed, the predominant impression is the idea of success. All his thoughts will therefore contain the elements of success, and the forces that can produce success; and he himself, will become thoroughly saturated with the very life of success. Nothing succeeds like success; therefore, the man that is filled with the spirit of success can never fail; and what is more, the forces that contain the elements of success will give that man the very qualifications that are essential to success, because like produces like. And again, the faculty required to produce the success desired, will be the one upon which all these success energies will be concentrated. When a man has the ability to do certain things, those things will be done; that is a foregone conclusion; and the ability to do what we want to do, comes when we constantly and persistently think that we can do what we want to do. In the mastery of fate, the law upon which this idea is based will be found indispensable;

because, since fate is created, and not controlled, all the elements of fate will have to be constantly recreated.

February 21st

Robert Collier

The way always opens for the determined soul, the man of faith and courage. —It is the victorious mental attitude, the consciousness of power, the sense of mastership, that does the big things in this world. If you haven't this attitude, if you lack self-confidence, begin now to cultivate it. A highly magnetized piece of steel will attract and lift a piece of unmagnetized steel ten times its own weight. Demagnetize that same piece of steel and it will be powerless to attract or lift even a feather's weight. Now, my friends, there is the same difference between the man who is highly magnetized by a sublime faith in himself, and the man who is demagnetized by his lack of faith, his doubts, his fears, that there is between the magnetized and the demagnetized pieces of steel. If two men of equal ability, one magnetized by a divine self-confidence, the other demagnetized by fear and doubt, are given similar tasks, one will succeed and the other will fail. The self-confidence of the one multiplies his powers a hundred-fold; the lack of it subtracts a hundred-fold from the power of the other."

February 22nd

Ernest Holmes

Whoever touches truth, no matter in what generation, will always get the same answer. The great truth that was revealed from Moses to the time of Jesus is the same truth that is still revealed to all who will accept it; it is simply this: we are now living in a Spiritual Universe governed by mental laws of cause and effect. Moses saw it mostly from the standpoint of the Law of cause and effect, an eye for an eye. What does this mean? It means, as Jesus said, "As a man sows, so shall he reap." Moses saw the law. Jesus saw not only the law ("I AM come not to destroy but to fulfill"), but he saw behind the law the reason for it, and revealed behind all law the Great Law-giver, a God of love working out the great inner concepts of His own being in harmony and in beauty, filled with peace, causing the sun to shine alike upon the just and the unjust. Jesus did not try to overcome the use of law; He understood all law and He well knew that all law was at His command; He did not break the law.

February 23rd

Joseph Murphy

The tomb of Hermes was opened with great expectancy and a sense of wonder because people believed that the greatest secret of the ages was contained therein. The secret was as within, so without; as above, so below. In other words, whatever is impressed in your subconscious mind is expressed on the screen of space. This same truth was proclaimed by Moses, Isaiah, Jesus, Buddha, Zoroaster, Lao Tzu, and all the illumined seers of the ages Whatever you feel as true subjectively is expressed as conditions, experiences, and events. Motion and emotion must balance. As in heaven [your own mind], so on earth [in your body and environment]. This is the great law of life.

February 24th

Joseph Murphy

Your subconscious mind accepts what is impressed upon it or what you consciously believe. It does not reason things out like your conscious mind, and it does not argue with you controversially. Your subconscious mind is like the soil, which accepts any kind of seed, good or bad. Your thoughts are active and might be likened unto seeds. Negative, destructive thoughts continue to work negatively in your subconscious mind, and in due time will come forth into outer experience which corresponds with them. Remember, your subconscious mind does not engage in proving whether your thoughts are good or bad, true or false, but it responds according to the nature of your thoughts or suggestions.

February 25th

Prentice Mulford

A condition of mind can be brought on you resulting to you in good or ill, sickness or health, or poverty or wealth, by the action, conscious or unconscious of other minds about you, and also through the thought suggested you by objects or scenes about you. This is the secret of what in former times was called the " spell." Through the action of thought a state of mind can be brought on any person which may make them act conformably to such thought. The "spell" is a matter of everyday occurrence in some form or other. To remain for an hour in sight of grand scenery casts on the mind a "spell" of pleasurable thought. To remain for an hour in a vault surrounded by coffins and skeletons would, through the associations connected with such objects, cast on you a " spell" of gloom. To live for days and weeks in a family, all of whose members hated you or were prejudiced against you, would most likely cast on you a "spell" of depression and unpleasant sensation. To live in a family whose members were always sending you warm and friendly thought would place a "spell" of pleasurable sensation. If when sick you are obliged to remain for days and possibly weeks in the same room, your mind will become weary of seeing continually the same objects in it. Not only is the mind wearied at sight of these objects, but the sight of each one, from day to day, will suggest the same train of thoughts, which also soon become wearisome. Mind weariness from this or any other cause has a natural drift towards despondency. Matters present and future then assume their darkest aspect and the darkest side of every possibility comes uppermost. Despondent thought, as has been many times repeated, is force used to tear the body down instead of building it up. This action and condition of thought is one form of the "spell." This is quickest broken by a change to another place and another room.

February 26th

Christian Larson

The principal reason why a man who is down, remains there, and continues to appear as ordinary as his environment, is because he permits his mind to be impressed with everything that his environment may suggest. His thoughts are therefore the reflections of his surroundings, and he is like his thoughts. Therefore, the man who would become different from his environment must learn the art of original thinking, and must enter the attitude of self-supremacy. The principal reason why a man is underpaid is because he does not value himself, and therefore hides behind personal inferiority the greater part of his ability. Another reason is because he works only for the wages that are coming to himself. He refuses to do more than is absolutely necessary, lest someone might be benefited. This attitude produces the cramped condition, which in turn reacts upon the purse. The man who is afraid to do too much, usually fails to do enough; at any rate, he produces that impression, and his recompense is lowered accordingly. On the other hand, the man who does his best at all times, regardless of the scale of wages, not only produces an excellent impression everywhere, but makes those in authority feel that he wants the enterprise to succeed. He is therefore better paid, because such men are valuable. They are wanted everywhere, not because they do more than they are paid for, but because they are a living power for success wherever they are called upon to act. The spirit of success breeds success; and the man who takes a living interest in the enterprise for which he works, even doing more than he is expected to do when the occasion demands, is creating the spirit of success, and will soon share in the greater success that follows.

February 27th

Charles F. Haanel

Thought contains a vital principle, because it is the creative principle of the Universe and by its nature will combine with other similar thoughts. As the one purpose of life is growth, all principles underlying existence must contribute to give it effect. Thought, therefore, takes form and the law of growth eventually brings it into manifestation. You may freely choose what you think, but the result of your thought is governed by an immutable law. Any line of thought persisted in cannot fail to produce its result in the character, health and circumstances of the individual. Methods whereby we can substitute habits of constructive thinking for those which we have found produce only undesirable effects are therefore of primary importance. We all know that this is by no means easy. Mental habits are difficult to control, but it can be done and the way to do it is to begin at once to substitute constructive thought for destructive thought. Form the habit of analyzing every thought. If it is necessary, if its manifestation in the objective will be a benefit, not only to yourself, but to all whom it may affect in any way, keep it; treasure it; it is of value; it is in tune with the Infinite; it will grow and develop and produce fruit an hundred fold. On the other hand, it will be well for you to keep this quotation from George Matthews Adams, in mind, "Learn to keep the door shut, keep out of your mind, out of your office, and out of your world, every element that seeks admittance with no definite helpful end in view." If your thought has been critical or destructive, and has resulted in any condition of discord or inharmony in your environment, it may be necessary for you to cultivate a mental attitude which will be conducive to constructive thought. The imagination will be found to be a great assistance in this direction; the cultivation of the imagination leads to the development of the ideal out of which your future will emerge.

February 28th

Ernest Holmes

No one wants to associate with the dead. People are looking for a more abundant expression of life, not for depression and fault-finding. Find fault with no one, and more than this find no fault with yourself. Get over the thought of condemning people and things. People and things are all right; let them alone and enjoy life. Your very atmosphere will cheer and uplift the people who contact you, and a new life will enter into them.

February 29th (Leap Year)

Walter C. Lanyon

When you are once enveloped in the secrecy of the Spirit of the Presence, you will know why it is that "their shoes wax not old' and that the 'manna falls daily." "The whole creation groaneth" — to wit, for the redemption of the body. We see this redemption within ourselves. Verily this has been true to our blinded eyes. A world of people writhing and twisting, begging for mercy, seeking money, health, success, happiness; eternally seeking "things," and finding only ashes. The veil shall be torn from your eyes by the Spirit of the Consciousness of the Presence of God, and you shall see that the whole creation — your creation — your heaven — rejoiceth and maketh a glad sound, for the Redeemer has come into manifestation. Do you see? You who read this page? You?

March

March 1st

James Allen

Every man is where he is by the law of his being. The thoughts which he has built into his character have brought him there, and in the arrangement of his life there is no element of chance, but all is the result of a law which cannot err. This is just as true of those who feel "out of harmony" with their surroundings as of those who are contented with them. As the progressive and evolving being, man is where he is that he may learn that he may grow; and as he learns the spiritual lesson which any circumstance contains for him, it passes away and gives place to other circumstances.

March 2nd

Joseph Murphy

Your subconscious mind cannot argue controversially. Hence, if you give it wrong suggestions, it will accept them as true and will proceed to bring them to pass as conditions, experiences, and events. All things that have happened to you are based on thoughts impressed on your subconscious mind through belief. If you have conveyed erroneous concepts to your subconscious mind, the sure method of overcoming them is by the repetition of constructive, harmonious thoughts frequently repeated which your subconscious mind accepts, thus forming new and healthy habits of thought and life, for your subconscious mind is the seat of habit. The habitual thinking of your conscious mind establishes deep grooves in your subconscious mind. This is very favorable for you if your habitual thoughts are harmonious, peaceful, and constructive. If you have indulged in fear, worry, and other destructive forms of thinking, the remedy is to recognize the omnipotence of your subconscious mind and decree freedom, happiness, and perfect health. Your subconscious mind, being creative and one with your divine source, will proceed to create the freedom and happiness, which you have earnestly decreed.

March 3rd

Christian Larson

Every thought has creative power; and this power will express itself according to the desire that was in mind when the thought was created. Therefore, if every thought is to express its creative power in the building up of man, mind must constantly be filled with the spirit of that purpose. When the desire for growth and superior attainment does not predominate in mind, the greater part of the creative energy of thought will misdirect, and artificial mental conditions will form, only to act as obstacles to man's welfare and advancement. The creative power of thought is the only power employed in the construction and reconstruction of man; and for this reason man is as he thinks. Consequently, when man thinks what he desires to think, he will become what he desires to become. But to think what he desires to think, he must consciously govern the process through which impressions are formed upon mind. To govern this process is to have the power to exclude any impression from without that is not desired, and to completely impress upon mind every original thought that may be formed; thus giving mind the power to think only what it consciously chooses to think. Before man can govern this process, he must understand the difference between the two leading attitudes of mind the attitude of self-submission, and the attitude of self-supremacy; and must learn how to completely eliminate the former, and how to establish all life, all thought, and all action absolutely upon the latter. When this is done, no impression can form upon mind without man's conscious permission; and complete control of the creative power of thought is permanently secured. To master the creative power of thought is to master the personal self; and to master the personal self is to master fate.

March 4th

Ernest Holmes

There is too much struggle coming into the metaphysical thought. Often we hear some seeker after truth say, "I have a big fight ahead." O foolish and untaught, how can you hope to enter in! The kingdom comes not from without, but from within, always. Stop all struggle and wait upon the sure principle that creates whatever it wills because there is nothing to oppose it. As long as we think that opposition exists we are blocking the way for the clearer vision. Those that take up the sword must perish by it; not because God is a jealous God, but because that is the way the law must work.

March 5th

Venice J. Bloodworth

You have seen people work and strive for something and just when everything seemed coming their way the unexpected element stepped in and destroyed all their efforts. On the other hand, we see people who gain everything they wish with very little effort. Everything just seems to happen for them. It is the appearance of such things that leads people to believe that fate or luck worked for some and against others. The cause for every condition being thought and invisible is not taken into consideration. The effects, good or bad, may arise from any number of sources, but the cause had to originate in the mind of the individual affected. This is so true that you may gauge a man's mental capacities by taking stock of his physical condition and his immediate environment. The greatest barrier to individual progress is a slavish devotion to precedent. We do what everybody else does; we believe with the majority, without inquiring whether a doctrine is based on a myth or is a scientific fact. If these beliefs were transient mental impressions, no harm would be done, but when an idea sinks into the subconscious mind it comes forth as material results and while we do not realize it, we unconsciously fight any opposition to these submerged tendencies. That is the reason it is so hard to overcome a long established habit. The only way to overcome error is to know the truth; to know that mind is the only creator and that we may consciously create any condition in body and affairs by holding a mental picture of the desired condition.

The Within Creates The Without: Daily Meditations

March 6th

James Allen

Each man moves in the limited or expansive circle of his own thoughts, and all outside that circle is non-existent to him. He only knows that which he has become. The narrower the boundary, the more convinced is the man that there is no further limit, no other circle. The lesser cannot contain the greater, and he has no means of apprehending the larger minds; such knowledge comes only by growth. The man who moves in a widely extended circle of thought knows all the lesser circles from which he has emerged, for in the larger experience all lesser experiences are contained and preserved; and when his circle impinges upon the sphere of perfect manhood, when he is fitting himself for company and communion with them of blameless conduct and profound understanding, then his wisdom will have become sufficient to convince him that there are wider circles still beyond of which he is as yet but dimly conscious, or is entirely ignorant at the world of men and things, are looking into a mirror which gives back their own reflection.

March 7th

Robert Collier

Thirty years ago, Emile Coue electrified the world with his cures of all manner of disease. "Nobody ought to be sick!" he proclaimed, and proceeded to prove it by curing hundreds who came to him after doctors had failed to relieve them. Not only that, but he showed how the same methods could be used to cure one's affairs, to bring riches instead of debts, success instead of drudgery. What was back of his success? A law as old as the hills, a law that has been known to psychologists for years — the law that the subconscious mind accepts as TRUE anything that is repeated to it convincingly and often. And once it has accepted such a statement as true, it proceeds to do everything in its power to MAKE IT TRUE! You ask a friend how he is, and he carelessly answers — "I am sick, I am poor, I am unlucky," never stopping to think that by those very words he is fastening misfortune upon himself, suggesting to his subconscious mind that it proceed on the assumption that he IS sick or poor or weak or unfortunate. "Therefore I say unto you, what things soever ye desire when ye pray, believe that ye receive them, and ye shall HAVE them!"

March 8th

Charles F. Haanel

Thought is the connecting link between the Infinite and the finite, between the Universal and the individual. We have seen that there is an impassable barrier between the organic and the inorganic, and that the only way that matter can unfold is to be impregnated with life; as a seed reaches down into the mineral world and begins to unfold and reach out, the dead matter begins to live, a thousand invisible fingers begin to weave a suitable environment for the new arrival, and as the law of growth begins to take effect, we see the process continue until the Lily finally appears, and even "Solomon in all his glory was not arrayed like one of these". Even so, a thought is dropped into the invisible substance of the Universal Mind, that substance from which all things are created, and as it takes root, the law of growth begins to take effect and we find that conditions and environment are but the objective form of our thought. The law is that Thought is an active vital form of dynamic energy which has the power to correlate with its object and bring it out of the invisible substance from which all things are created into the visible or objective world. This is the law by which, and through which all things come into manifestation; it is the Master Key by which you are admitted into the Secret Place of the Most High and are "given dominion over all things." With an understanding of this law you may "decree a thing and it shall be established unto thee." It could not be otherwise; if the soul of the Universe as we know it is the Universal Spirit, then the Universe is simply the condition which the Universal Spirit has made for itself. We are simply individualized spirit and are creating the conditions for our growth in exactly the same way.

March 9th

Ernest Holmes

Man is surrounded by a great universal thought power which returns to him always just as he thinks. So plastic, so receptive is this mind, that it takes the slightest impression and moulds it into conditions. There are two things in man which his thought affects, his body and his environment. At all times he is given absolute control over these two things, and from the effect of his thought upon them he cannot hope to escape. At first, being ignorant of this fact, he binds himself by a misuse of the laws of his being; but as he begins to see that he himself is responsible for all that comes to him on the path of life, he begins to control his thought, which in its turn acts on the universal substance to create for him a new world.

March 10th

Christian Larson

There is more to live for than you ever imagined. Thus far most of us have only touched the merest surface of human existence; we are only on the verge of the splendor of life as it is; we are standing on the outside, so to speak, of the real mansion of mind and soul; and one reason is we live too much in the limitations of our disappointments, our lost opportunities, our blasted hopes, our vanquished dreams. We remain in that small world, deploring fate, when, if we would only permit mind and soul to take wings and go out upon the vastness of real existence, we would find, not only freedom, but a life infinitely richer than we had ever dreamed. But if mind and soul are to take wings in this fashion, we must learn to be glad. The heart that lives in disappointments is heavy. It will sink into the lowlands, and remain among the marshes and the bogs. But the glad heart ascends to the mountain tops. Therefore it is when we have such a heart that we can go out in search of new worlds, new opportunities, new possibilities, new joys. And the glad heart always finds that for which it goes in search. The reason is simple; for all things respond to the call of rejoicing; all things gather where life is a song. The great soul is always in search of ways and means for adding to the welfare of others. But no way is better, greater or more far-reaching than this, just be glad.

March 11th

Joseph Murphy

Life is livingness and givingness. Love is the outward flow of life; this flow must be harmonious, joyous, rhythmical, and peaceful. This cosmic urge must be expressed in a positive, constructive manner. Man must be in tune with the Infinite. He must find the thing he loves to do in life, and do it; then he will be happy. Such a man has a sense of freedom and joyous expectancy; he no longer watches the clock, but his joy is in accomplishment and service. Now his work is not drudgery; it is a pleasure.

March 12th

Uriel Buchanan

To know that the mind is the builder, that the mind is a concretion of the most potent forces of life, that thought is a dynamic power more potent than any possible opposing influence, will give you encouragement and strength to create nobler thoughts and to make use of your talents for the accomplishment of the greatest good. A chart should be hung in the room of every person who is working to develop the higher attributes of his nature, and on this chart should be printed in attractive letters the words and sentences which will suggest thoughts that will be specially helpful. To have the chart in a prominent place where your eyes will rest on it when you are meditating, and also during odd moments when your mind wanders from your book or writing or any work you are doing, the suggestions you will receive at such times will take hold of your thoughts and exert a beneficial influence in your daily life. To place before your mind, during the last hour of the evening and the early moments of the morning, whatever thought you desire to absorb in your nature, will aid you to develop corresponding attributes of character.

March 13th

Wallace Wattles

Guard your speech. Never speak of yourself, your affairs, or of anything else in a discouraged or discouraging way. Never admit the possibility of failure or speak in a way that infers failure as a possibility. Never speak of the times as being hard or of business conditions as being doubtful. Times may be hard and business doubtful for those who are on the competitive plane, but they can never be so for you. You can create what you want, and you are above fear. When others are having hard times and poor business, you will find your greatest opportunities. Train yourself to think of and to look upon the world as a something which is becoming, which is growing, and to regard seeming evil as being only that which is undeveloped. Always speak in terms of advancement. To do otherwise is to deny your faith, and to deny your faith is to lose it. Never allow yourself to feel disappointed. You may expect to have a certain thing at a certain time and not get it at that time, and this will appear to you like failure. But if you hold to your faith you will find that the failure is only apparent. Go on in the certain way, and if you do not receive that thing, you will receive something so much better that you will see that the seeming failure was really a great success.

March 14th

Ernest Holmes

The law obtains through all nature that as a man sows, so must he reap. Now the Father has brought us to where we can understand life, and we must go as we choose. If we are in harmony with the great forward movement of the Spirit, there is nothing that can hinder our advancement; if we oppose it, somewhere along our pathway it will crush us. As with individuals so with nations; in so far as they work with a right spirit they prosper; when they begin to fail in the use of this law they begin to fall. He who understands will take the position of one who wishes to work in union with the Power of Good; and to such an one will come all the power that he can conceive of and believe in; his word becomes in expression as the very word of God, and he must realize it to be all powerful. So the one who is truly united with Good will wish to express only the truth for all; and in doing so he is working along the lines of the unfoldment of the Spirit, and though he may seem to fail, from the ordinary standpoint, yet his success is assured; for he is at one with the only ultimate power before which, in time, all else must fall.

March 15th

Robert Collier

No one has failed as long as he can begin again. So start now to do the things you feel you have it in you to do. Ask permission of no man. Your belief that you can do the thing gives your thought-force their power. Fortune waits upon you. Seize her boldly, hold her and she is yours. She belongs rightfully to you. The men who have made their mark in this world all had one trait in common — they believed in themselves. So what do you want most from life? Whatever it is, you can have it — if you can believe in it — if you can see in it in your mind's eye as yours. You must be able to hold it in your thought, visualize it, see yourself having it. You must make your model clear-cut and distinct.

1. Remember, the first thing necessary is a sincere desire, concentrating your thought on one thing with singleness of purpose.

2. The second is visualization, seeing yourself doing it, imaging the object in the same way that God first imaged everything He created.

3. The third essential is to take whatever action is necessary to start your nucleus revolving and growing.

4. Next is faith, believing that you HAVE the thing you want, affirming constantly to your image in the mirror that you

ARE rich or successful or healthy or happy. Not that you are going to be, mind you but that you ARE!

5. And the last is gratitude, gratitude for this thing that you have received, for the power that enabled you to create it, for all the gifts that Mind has given you in such profusion. Thank God that you HAVE received.

March 16th

Christian Larson

Whatever comes or not, sing again and again the song of "the soul victorious"; and mean it with your whole heart. Enter into this song with all the power of mind and spirit, for it is always that which we know and sincerely believe that contains the greater worth and power. When you resolve to be glad at all times and under every circumstance, resolve also to give your whole heart and soul to the spirit of your rejoicing. Give power to your gladness, and give life to your song. Open the way for all the sunshine of your soul; and see that every sunbeam from within be one of power as well as one of joy. It is the full joy of the soul that makes the heart young and the mind great. For as it is in nature, so it is also in man. It is the full glory of the noonday sun that quickens the earth, that makes the fields green, that causes the flowers to bloom. Where the sun is strong all growth is luxurious and all nature bountiful. It is the same when the sunshine of the soul is full, strong and constant in the daily life of man. So therefore rejoice with great joy. Rejoice always and give life and power to your joy.

March 17th

Prentice Mulford

If you in your mind are ever building an ideal of yourself as strong, healthy, and vigorous, you are building to yourself of invisible element that which is ever drawing to you more of health, strength, and vigor. You can make of your mind a magnet to attract health or weakness. If you love to think of the strong things in Nature, of granite mountains and heaving billows and resistless tempests, you attract to you their elements of strength. If you build yourself in health and strength today, and despond and give up such thinking or building tomorrow, you do not destroy what in spirit and of spirit you have built up. That amount of element so added to your spirit can never be lost; but you do, for the time, in so desponding, that is, thinking weakness, stop the building of your health structure; and although your spirit is so much the stronger for that addition of element, it may not be strong enough to give quickly to the body what you may have taken from it through such despondent thought. Persistency in thinking health, in imagining or idealizing yourself as healthy, vigorous, and symmetrical, is the cornerstone of health and beauty. Of that which you think most, that you will be, and that you will have most of. You say, "No." But your bed-ridden patient is not thinking, "I AM strong;" he or she is thinking," I am so weak." Your dyspeptic man or woman is not thinking, "I will have a strong stomach." They are ever saying, "I can't digest anything;" and they can't, for that very reason.

March 18th

Venice J. Bloodworth

The Laws of Life and Nature do not punish or reward man. We simply live in or out of harmony with Nature's Laws and our happiness or misery, health or disease, prosperity or poverty, is the working out of the Law as cause and effect in perfect harmony with our individual demands. This is the truth that we must understand and live by if peace, power, love, health, happiness, and success are to be a part of our daily life. THE ONLY WAY TO CHANGE YOUR CONDITIONS IN LIFE IS TO CHANGE YOUR MIND ABOUT LIFE. The road to happiness and prosperity begins in one's secret thoughts, and the motive power by which we progress along that road is constructive emotion expressed in right action.

March 19th

Ernest Holmes

There is a subtle danger in using denials; we may deny to such an extent as to erect a barrier or build a mountain to overcome. Once realize that God makes things out of Himself simply by speaking, and you will never again use denials in treating. All that needs changing is the false thought, and by affirming that your word destroys everything but itself you will embody all that a denial could. In those systems that teach denials we find that the more enlightened ones are gradually using the affirmative method, and as this is the growth of experience there can be no doubt that it is the better method. Of one thing we may be sure, the Spirit never denies. It simply knows that I AM.

March 20th

Eugene Del Mar

The Universal Principle of Attraction is rooted alike in Justice and Love. Because the Universe is dominated by an All-inclusive Principle, all truths are contrasting manifestations of the One Truth. Infinite Justice and Infinite Love have identical meanings. The popular conceptions of justice and of love place them in contrast and opposition. Love is thought to be warm and justice cold, the one typifying life and the other death. Love is regarded as expressing emotion, justice the lack of it. Love suggests giving, while justice implies withholding. The contrast between one's conceptions of love and justice depends primarily on whether he is looking from the universal or the individual viewpoint, whether he is taking the larger or the smaller view. There is an exact relation between cause and effect. Each individual may determine what he shall sow. He may reap whatever he desire. When he sows the right seed and cares for it after sowing, he may produce any effect through putting in operation the cause with which it is correlated. And any effect must continue unless its cause is modified, changed or altered. The seeds one sows are his thoughts and acts. These are influenced largely by the environments that his prior thoughts and acts have caused to be related to him. As he changes his thoughts, he impels a change of environment which in turn induces new thought-combinations. Through right living one acquires a constantly increasing ability consciously to fashion and determine his environment, and harmoniously to adjust himself to it. With a developed understanding of the relation between cause and effect one consciously produces the results he desires. Knowing the seed he sows, he is certain of the harvest. Not only does he receive what he deserves, and that to which he is entitled, but knowing this to be true he is conscious of eternal justice, and his perception ripens into abiding realization of the love and harmony of the Universe.

March 21st

James Allen

Man is not bound by any power outside his own wrong thoughts, and from these he can set himself free; and foremost, the enslaving thoughts from which he needs to be delivered are I cannot rise, I cannot break away from bad habits, I cannot alter my nature, I cannot control and conquer myself, I CANNOT CEASE FROM SIN. All these cannots have no existence in the things to which they submit; they exist only in thought. Such negations are bad thought-habits which need to be eradicated, and in their place should be planted the positive I can which should be tended and developed until it becomes a powerful tree of habit, bearing the good and life-giving fruit of right and happy living.

March 22nd

Christian Larson

Just be glad, even though the whole world be against you, and all the elements of nature be in a conspiracy to place you in the hands of destruction. Even at such a time, just be glad. Thus you prove your strength. And he who can prove that he is stronger than any adversary, will win the respect yes, and the friendship, of every adversary. What was against you will be for you. And this was your secret you refused to be downcast, you refused to weaken, you refused to be less than your greatest self even when everything seemed lost, you were strong enough to be true to all that you knew to be true, and you tuned your life to the music of that sweetest of all refrains just be glad. Because you were glad, even when there was nothing to make you glad, you proved that you deserved everything that has the power to make you glad. And that which we truly deserve must come to remain as our own. Just be glad. Whether there is anything to be glad for or not, just be glad. It is the royal path to happiness. It is the royal path to all that is worthy and beautiful in life. Above all things, possess gladness, and you will soon possess those things that produce gladness. Be your own sunbeam, and you will attract a million sunbeams. Be your own source of your own joy, and you will attract everything and everybody that can add to your joy. To him that hath shall be given. And he already hath who has found the riches of his own nature. To find those riches is the first step. All else must follow. All other things will be added. And to find those riches, use well every talent you possess. Then whatever comes, just be glad. For all things respond to the call of rejoicing; all things gather where life is a song.

March 23rd

Joseph Murphy

On Healing

There are a great number who claim that because their theory produces results, it is, therefore, the correct one; this, as explained in this chapter, cannot be true. You know there are all types of healing. Mesmer and others healed by claiming they were sending forth a certain magnetic fluid. Other men came along and said all of this was nonsense, that the healing was due to suggestion. All of these groups, such as psychiatrists, psychologists, osteopaths, chiropractors, physicians, and all churches are using the one universal, healing power resident in the subconscious mind. Each may proclaim the healings are due to their theory. The process of all healing is a definite, positive, mental attitude, an inner certitude, or a way of thinking called faith. Healing is due to a confident expectancy which acts as a powerful suggestion to the subconscious mind releasing its healing potency. One man does not heal by a different power than another. It is true he may have his own theory and method. There is only one process of healing, and that is faith; there is only one healing power, namely, your subconscious mind. Select the theory and method which you prefer. You can rest assured, if you have the faith, you shall get results.

March 24th

Ernest Holmes

What is the Spirit, anyway? We all answer, "Why of course, it is God." Where is the Spirit? It is present at all times and in all places. True spirituality must simply mean coming to realize the presence of this Spirit. It must be coming to rely upon it more than anything else. The one then who is the most spiritual is simply the one who relies the most; that is all. No matter where he is, he must rely, he must trust, he must believe. We do not have to give up anything but negative thought and act. We do not want to do anything that contradicts the forward march of the unfoldment of the Spirit, so all that we think and do must be in line with that which is right. But who shall say what is and what is not right? Remember this forever, only your own soul shall say what is right and what is wrong. "To thine own self be true, and it shall follow as the night the day, thou canst not then be false to any man." Look to no one for guidance. This is the "blind leading the blind." The Almighty has put the truth into your own soul; look there and there alone for it.

March 25th

Henry Thomas Hamblin

Whatever you create in your mental world by means of visualizing will in time be manifested in the outer physical world. The outer world of matter is subservient to the inner world of mind. This is a great occult truth which has been withheld from ordinary people and has been until recently the closely guarded secret of certain secret orders. It is now given into your hands, you are put upon your honor not to reveal it to others. When they have reached a certain stage of their development, the knowledge will come to them by some channel or other, and in the meantime it does more harm than good to try to impart occult knowledge to those who are not interested or ready to receive it. I hope enough has been said to arouse your interest in, and enthusiasm for, visualizing. The more clearly you can visualize, the more clean cut will be the results in your daily life. This creative power can be so highly developed that a sick man can make himself well, a poor man can change his circumstances from poverty to prosperity, and a miserable and despondent pessimist can change himself into a cheery, optimist. By visualizing, and by denials and affirmations (which will be explained later), by meditation and by the exercise of Hope and Faith the life, character and circumstances can be transformed. The results are so extraordinary that it is very difficult to get people to believe them, but they are none the less real. Therefore practice your affirmations and persevere with your visualizing, they will lead to results of which you can at present form but a faint conception.

March 26th

Uriel Buchanan

How often we meet with difficulties which oppress the heart and cause the will to waver, when we might arise in the dignity of selfhood and speak the word which would set free the latent energies of the mind and will and give power to conquer all things which bar the way to liberty and progress. We are swayed by the hypnotic suggestions which other minds project, and we yield to the binding influence of race beliefs which we have inherited from the generations of the past, so that the highest part of our nature sleeps, not dreamlessly, but as one fettered by the chain of circumstances which he cannot break. Have an undoubting assurance that deep in yourself abides the unlimited power which will give mastery over every possible condition of material environment. Have no apprehension of evil, or impending misfortune; for what appears evil, which you may encounter on life's highway, will never be greater than the strength which you possess for protection. Though you may pass through troublous times, let fear be unknown to your heart. If the mind be inspired by the principles of goodness and truth, all that shall happen to you will be fraught with blessings; and looking through the mists of the uncertain future, you will see where the waves of seeming adversity break on the final shores with a murmur that awakens the echo, "All is well."

March 27th

Floyd B. Wilson

If one wants to master in a limited time a language, or any subject, he must secure a competent teacher and give the proper time to it. If he wishes to develop himself by methods which in the East have been known long, and which in the West are just beginning to be understood, he must find the time and go there in faith with purpose fixed, and work as all must work. The advanced students in modern psychology have learned that the Hindu taught a great metaphysical truth in regard to the development of man when he named the silence the hall of learning. I claim, however, that great advancement will be made while one is traveling on the path leading to the hall of silence. It will take weeks and months, and possibly years, of discipline to reach the inner chambers of the silence; and when one does, he there blends himself with the Universal, and he will then understand clearly his oneness with all life. THE DAWNING OF LIGHT.

March 28th

Christian Larson

Among the underpaid, by far the largest number is composed of those who submit absolutely to their present conditions, and therefore remain not only in bondage to unscrupulous taskmasters, but also to their own environments and mental limitations. They are the many weak, of whom some of the strong take advantage; and it is in behalf of these that reformers demand a change in the order of things. But it is not a change in the order of things that the world requires; it is a change of mind. And when the change of mind is produced, all other necessary changes will inevitably follow. If you are underpaid because you have submitted to the power of the unscrupulous, cease to live in the attitude of mental submission. Do not antagonize the powers to which you have submitted, and do not resist your present condition. In your external life continue as usual for a period; but change absolutely your internal life. What we resist we fear; and we always continue in bondage to that which we fear. What we antagonize, we meet on the inferior side, and thus enter into contact with the very things we desire to avoid. We shall never get rid of the inferior so long as we resist the inferior; and whatever stays with us will impress our minds. Therefore, by resisting the inferior, we produce inferiority in ourselves. Begin your emancipation by removing your attitude of self-submission; cease to believe that you must remain down where you are. Change your mind; know that inherently you are master over everything in your own domain, and resolve to exercise your supremacy. Refuse to be impressed by your environment; and learn to impress your own mind with superior impressions only. Recreate your own mind according to a higher standard of power, ability and character; thus you will recreate both yourself and your surroundings; because by making yourself stronger and more competent, you will be wanted where surroundings are better, and recompense greater.

March 29th

Ernest Holmes

The first thing to realize is that since any thought manifests it necessarily follows that all thought does the same, else how should we know that the particular thought we were thinking would be the one that would create? Mind must cast back all or none. Just as the creative power of the soil receives all seeds put into it, and at once begins to work upon them, so mind must receive all thought and at once begin to operate upon it. Thus we find that all thought has some power in our lives and over our conditions. We are making our environments by the creative power of our thought. God has created us thus and we cannot escape it. By conforming our lives and thought to a greater understanding of law we shall be able to bring into our experience just what we wish, letting go of all that we do not want to experience and taking in the things we desire.

March 30th

Prentice Mulford

We are through our mental conditions always drawing things to us good or bad, beneficial or injurious, pleasant or disagreeable. There is possible a state of mind which, if permanently kept, will draw to you money, lands, possessions, luxuries, health and happiness. It is a mental condition always serene, calm, determined, decided, self-composed, and bent on some purpose whose aim is lasting good, first to yourself, next to others. There is another state of mind which, if permanently kept in, will drive prosperity and health from you. It is only the very small part of what exists in the universe that can be seen, touched or otherwise made evident to the physical senses. The larger part of what exists and has form, shape and color, cannot be seen, felt or be otherwise made evident to the physical senses. What we call space is filled with realities. There is no such thing as "empty space." These realities might be evident to our spiritual or finer senses were they developed. As these finer senses are more and more opened, then more and more of these things or realities will become evident to us. Whatever you think you actually make. You are making these unseen realities continually as you think. If you think of anything but a second you make that an unseen reality for a second. If you think of it for hours, days and years, you will in some way bring that reality to you in the physical world. If you keep any idea good or ill in your mind from month to month and year to year, you make it a more enduring unseen reality, and as it so becomes stronger and stronger, it must at last take shape and appear in the seen and physical.

March 31st

Floyd B. Wilson

There are today in the various cities of the world, cults or societies which call their members together daily at a certain hour for silence. There each holds in his mind the desire of his heart, or the desire to aid someone in a particular way, or holds himself absolutely passive that he as an instrument may receive or give, as the Universal wills. These societies report the steady and continuous unfoldment of their members, unfoldment to attain happiness, unfoldment to advance mental growth, unfoldment to understand, step by step, more and more of what human life may mean.

April

April 1st

James Allen

If we fear our fellow-men, fear opinion, poverty, the withdrawal of friends and influence, then we are bound indeed, and cannot know the inward happiness of the enlightened, the freedom of the just; but if in our thoughts we are pure and free, if we see in life's reactions and reverses nothing to cause us trouble or fear, but everything to aid us in our progress, nothing remains that can prevent us from accomplishing the aims of our life, for then we are free indeed.

April 2nd

Joseph Murphy

Begin now to believe and claim that money is wonderful. Begin to love money and be friendly with it; you will always have plenty; you will never want. Love is an emotional attachment. Except you love your work, or profession, you cannot be a true success. Love always magnifies and multiplies. Love the, idea of wealth until it becomes embodied subjectively. Write this down in big letters in your mind: What you love, you increase. What you criticize, fades out of your life.

April 3rd

Ernest Holmes

Power is, and mind is, and life is; but they have to flow through us in order to express in our lives. We are dealing with law; and nature must be obeyed before it will work for us. Just realize that this law is as natural a law as any other of God's laws, and use it with the same intelligence that you would use the law of electricity; then you will get the desired results. We provide the thought form around which the divine energies play and to which they attract the conditions necessary for the fulfillment of the thought.

April 4th

Robert Collier

Our railroads, our telephones, our automobiles, our libraries, our newspapers, our thousands of other conveniences, comforts and necessities are due to the creative genius of but two per cent of our population. And the same two per cent own a great percentage of the wealth of the country. The question arises, Who are they? What are they? The sons of the rich? College men? No — few of them had any early advantages. Many of them have never seen the inside of a college. It was grim necessity that drove them, and somehow, some way, they found a method of drawing upon their Creative Force, and through that Force they reached success. You don't need to stumble and grope. You can call upon the Creative Force at will. There are three steps necessary: First, to realize that you have the power. Second, to know what you want. Third, to center your thought upon it with singleness of purpose. To accomplish these steps takes only a fuller understanding of the Power-that-is-within-you.

April 5th

Christian Larson

To make real the ideal, the first essential is to remove from consciousness the gulf that seems to exist between present attainment and the greater possibilities. Refuse to think of this gulf, because to think of it is to impress the mind with the idea that the greater is beyond us. This impression will prevent mind from reaching the greater, and will also produce frequent states of despair. Such states not only weaken mind, but cause man to give himself up to the influence of environment. A discouraged mind, submitting itself to environment, is impressed with failure, weakness, inferiority, and the tendency to go down grade; while the mind that is to master fate must go the other way. To remove the seeming gulf from mind, turn attention not only upon the ideal you desire to reach, but try to see the ideal of yourself as well. By so doing you impress the ideal of yourself upon your mind; thoughts like the ideal self will be created, and your personal self becomes like the thoughts you think. Consequently, by a simple process, the personal self is made to improve constantly, daily becoming more and more like the ideal. To realize constant personal advancement is to prevent all thoughts of discouragement, and also to enter the power of that law through which gain promotes gain, and much gathers more. The law is that you begin to realize the ideal in your personal life when the personal self begins to grow into the likeness of the ideal. Therefore, to yearn for ideals while nothing is being done to make yourself more ideal, is to continue to keep yourself away from your ideal. It is like that attracts like, and only those who are alike will be drawn into the same world; consequently, to live in the same world with your ideal, you must become like your ideal. The ideal cannot come down to you; ideals never move that way; but you can go up to your ideal, and that is the true way for you to move.

April 6th

Venice J. Bloodworth

Ye shall know the Truth and the Truth shall make you free. This is the age of mind; the age of inquiry; the age of discovery; and the greatest discovery of all the ages is the discovery of thought force and the power of thought. This great fact is as yet unknown to the majority of mankind. Too long have we been taught to look without for help, while the mighty power of our subconscious mind has been used ignorantly or not used at all while we struggle along on our surface power, which means that we are using about ten percent of our mentality, for ninety percent of our mental power is subconscious. In using this ten percent we deal with effects, looking always to the evidence of the five senses, while the marvelous powers and uses of Idealization, Visualization, Concentration and Realization are completely ignored. Is it any wonder that we find sickness, poverty and misery on every hand when we ignore the cause and deal always with effects? The visible material things have no originating power within themselves. Everything we see is the result of an idea; and we must REALIZE this truth before we can rise above and free ourselves from any condition.

Environment of any description is the manifestation of ideas. If the conditions are unsatisfactory, build new conditions in your mind, ignore the present surroundings and hold fast to your mental picture. THE REALIZATION OF YOUR POWER TO DO THIS IS THE TRUTH THAT MAKES MEN FREE.

April 7th

Ernest Holmes

When we look into the creative way of the spirit we find it impossible for denial to enter, as the Spirit recognizes no opposite to its own nature. It knows that "I AM and beside me there is no other." The Spirit does not deny anything, it simply affirms itself to be that which it desires to be. Seeing and recognizing no opposite to itself, it finds no need of denial, indeed, this thought need not enter the mind; if we are working with the Spirit we need not deny but state the affirmative attitude of mind, realizing that we are dealing with the only power that exists.

April 8th

Uriel Buchanan

Whatever suggestion is accepted by the mind we make a reality. We give it strength and activity. If we invite feelings of anxiety, fear, hatred and discouragement, we give such things vitality. If we hold to aspiring, cheerful, uplifting thoughts, the good within us will thrive, and create an intelligence of harmony. It is always our duty to nourish and cultivate only the true and good. The only hope of freedom from fear, grief, anxiety, disappointment and failure is in alertness and watchfulness. You should awaken harmonious living pictures which will inspire to noble effort and high aspiration. You should rise above morbid conditions and invoke the support of principles which are immutable and divine. You should be alone with yourself as much as possible, for concentration and individual aspiration. The problems of your life should be thought over and worked out in contemplation and solitude. At such times your mind will be free from the influence of others. Force yourself to think of some worthy achievement, until the memory of the thing sinks deep into your mind. Hold persistently to an intense special desire for the accomplishment of some noble aim. This attitude of mind will stir the divine nature within. By the quiet intensity of a determined resolve you will arouse a magnetic, nervous fire of energy which will execute your purpose against all odds.

April 9th

Prentice Mulford

The longer you put your mind on any one thing, be it evil or good, the stronger do you make it as an unseen reality. It must at last, as you keep it in mind or put your mind on it, make itself in the seen and physical world an agency for pain or pleasure. The power to fix mind persistently on some definite purpose, or in a certain frame or mood — say that of calm determination, or to keep mind from being disturbed, is not now very common. Look at many people about you. On what from year to year is their thought or purpose fixed? On getting their wages at the week's end. Beyond this nothing. On getting a new bonnet, a new dress, a pleasure trip. Beyond this nothing. On living from day to day, or week to week. Beyond this nothing. Many cannot fix their mind on any useful purpose for two days in succession. It is this thing earnestly desired today, something else tomorrow. Their mental forces pull a little while on this thing, abandon it, then pull a little on the next whim or fancy and abandon that. There is no steady pull or exercise of drawing power on any one thing. These are the people who accomplish very little, who are always poor, and often in ill health. These minds where fixed at all are often on the useless, and injurious. They will read with avidity of horrors and hangings. The longer these are spun out and the more minute are they in detail, the more they like them. They love the drama depicting violence or emotional torture. A vast amount of their force goes in this direction. It is a force to draw to them some form of evil. If turned in another direction it would draw to them good. The unseen world and upper currents of unseen realities are full of bright and beautiful things — full of the spiritual correspondences of all luxuries, necessities and good things enjoyed here — full of beautiful things as yet here never seen and enjoyed. When minds here learn, as in time they will, to have faith in these existences, and faith in the simple means of attracting them, they will fix their thought persistently on the bright side of life. They will come to know that the longer they endeavor so to fix it on the brighter and healthier side, the more power will they have, and the less effort will it cost so to keep their thought in the right direction and in connection with the right current, until at last it will become " second nature" for them to live in these higher realities, and, as so living, health and prosperity will flow toward them. They will cease then to think so much and read so much, and talk and live so much in the crude, the horrible, the long-drawn recitals of crime, having learned that these thoughts bring them evil and injure their power for drawing to them that which will result in permanent good. "Set your affections on things above." This upper current of thought contains the correspondences in unseen element of all that is good for us to use and enjoy, and more still of joys we do not yet realize. These are the "things above." Calm demand brings all good things in time. Impatient demand drives them away.

April 10th

Robert Collier

The greatest shortcut to prosperity is to LIVE IT! Prosperity attracts. Poverty repels. To quote Orison Swett Marden — "To be ambitious for wealth and yet always expecting to be poor, to be always doubting your ability to get what you long for, is like trying to reach East by travelling West. There is no philosophy which will help a man to succeed when he is always doubting his ability to do so, and thus attracting failure." Again: "No matter how hard you may work for success, if your thought is saturated with the fear of failure it will kill your efforts, neutralize your endeavors, and make success impossible." The secret of prosperity lies in so vividly imaging it in your own mind that you literally exude prosperity. You feel prosperous, you look prosperous, and the result is that before long you ARE prosperous.

April 11th

Ernest Holmes

The man who has learned to love all people, no matter who they may be, will find plenty of people who will return that love to him. This is not mere sentiment, and it is more than a religious attitude of mind; it is a deep scientific fact, and one to which we should pay attention. The reason is this: As all is mind, and as we attract to us what we first become, until we learn to love we are not sending out love vibrations, and not until we send out love vibrations can we receive love in return. One of the first things to do is to learn to love everybody. If you have not done this, begin to do so at once. There is always more good than bad in people, and seeing the good tends to bring it forth. Love is the greatest healing and drawing power on earth. It is the very reason for our being, and that explains why it is that people should have something or somebody to love.

April 12th

Christian Larson

Everything has a tendency to grow in the subconscious. Whenever an impression or desire is placed in the subconscious, it has a tendency to become larger and therefore the bad becomes worse when it enters the subconscious, while the good becomes better. We have the power, however, to exclude the bad from the subconscious and cause only the good to enter that immense field. Whenever you say that you are tired and permit that feeling to sink into the subconscious, you will almost at once feel more tired. Whenever you feel sick and permit that feeling to enter the subconscious, you always feel worse. The same is true when you are weak, sad, disappointed or depressed. If you let those feelings sink into your subconscious, they will become worse. On the other hand, when we feel happy, strong, persistent and determined, and permit those feelings to enter the subconscious, we always feel better. It is therefore highly important that we positively refuse to give in to any undesirable feeling. Whenever we give in to any feeling, it becomes subconscious, and if that feeling is bad, it becomes worse; but so long as we keep undesirable feelings on the outside, so to speak, we will hold them at bay, until nature can readjust itself or gather reserve force and thus put them out of the way altogether.

April 13th

Joseph Murphy

Here is a simple technique which you can follow: Quiet the mind; still the body; tell the body to relax; it has to obey you. It has no volition, initiative, or intelligence of itself; it is an emotional disc which records your beliefs and impressions. Immobilize your attention; focus your thought on the solution to your problem. Try and solve it with your conscious mind. Think how happy you would be about the perfect solution. If your mind wanders, bring it back gently. In this sleepy, drowsy state, say quietly and positively, "The answer is mine now; I know my subconscious mind knows the answer." Live now in the mood or feeling of the solution. Sense the feeling you would have if the perfect answer were yours now. Let your mind play with this mood in a relaxed way; then drop off to sleep. You may fall asleep sooner than you expected, but you were thinking about the answer; the time was not wasted. When you awaken, and you do not have the answer, get busy about something else. Probably when you are preoccupied with something else the answer will come into your mind, like toast pops out of the toaster.

April 14th

Wallace Wattles

Getting rich is not a matter of environment, for if it were, all the people in certain neighborhoods would become wealthy. The people of one city would all be rich, while those of other towns would all be poor, or all the inhabitants of one state would roll in wealth, while those of an adjoining state would be in poverty. But everywhere we see rich and poor living side by side, in the same environment, and often engaged in the same vocations. When two people are in the same locality and in the same business, and one gets rich while the other remains poor, it shows that getting rich is not primarily a matter of environment. Some environments may be more favorable than others, but when two people in the same business are in the same neighborhood and one gets rich while the other fails, it indicates that getting rich is the result of doing things in a certain way. And further, the ability to do things in this certain way is not due solely to the possession of talent, for many people who have great talent remain poor, while others who have very little talent get rich. Studying the people who have gotten rich, we find that they are an average lot in all respects, having no greater talents and abilities than other people have. It is evident that they do not get rich because they possess talents and abilities that others do not have, but because they happen to do things in a certain way.

April 15th

Ernest Holmes

Just imagine yourself surrounded by mind, so plastic, so receptive, that it receives the slightest impression of your thought. Whatever you think it takes up and executes for you. Every thought is received and acted upon. Not some but all thoughts. Whatever the pattern we provide, that will be our demonstration. If we cannot get over thinking that we are poor then we will still remain poor. As soon as we become rich in our thought then we will be rich in our expression. These are not mere words, but the deepest truth that has ever come to the human race. Hundreds of thousands of the most intelligent thinkers and the most spiritual people of our day are proving this truth. We are not dealing with illusions but with realities; pay no more attention to the one who ridicules these ideas than you would to the blowing of the wind.

April 16th

Genevieve Behrend

In the conscious uses of the Universal Power to reproduce your desires in physical form, three facts should be borne in mind:

First — All space is filled with a Creative Power.

Second — This Creative Power is amenable to suggestion.

Third — It can only work by deductive methods.

As Troward tells us, this last is an exceedingly important point, for it implies that the action of the ever-present Creative Power is in no way limited by precedent. It works according to the essence of the spirit of the principle. In other words, this Universal Power takes its creative direction from the word you give it. Once man realizes this great truth, the character with which this sensitive, reproductive power is invested becomes the most important of all his considerations. It is the unvarying law of Creative Life Principle that "As a man thinketh in his heart, so is he." If you realize the truth that the Creative Power can be to you only what you feel and think it to be, it is willing and able to meet your demands. Troward says, "If you think your thought is Powerful, your Thought is Powerful."

April 17th

James Allen

Thus each man is an accumulation of thoughts and deeds. The characteristics which he manifests instinctively and without effort are lines of thought and action become, by long repetition, automatic; for it is the nature of habit to become, at last, unconscious, to repeat, as it were, itself without any apparent choice or effort on the part of its possessor; and in due time it takes such complete possession of the individual as to appear to render his will powerless to counteract it. This is the case with all habits, whether good or bad; when bad, the man is spoken of as being the victim" of a bad habit or a vicious mind; when good, he is referred to as having, by nature, a good disposition".

April 18th

Christian Larson

The great majority are receiving all sorts of suggestions every hour, and they respond to a very large number of them; in fact, we can truthfully say that most people are controlled, most of the time, by suggestions that come to them from their environment. Those minds, however, who understand the power of thought, and who know the difference between detrimental and beneficial suggestions, can close their minds to the former and open them fully to the latter. And the method to apply is this, that whenever you are in the presence of an adverse suggestion, concentrate your attention upon some idea or mental state which you know will act as a counter suggestion; in other words, when adverse suggestion is trying to produce in your mind what you do not want, persist in suggesting to yourself what you do want. This practice, if employed frequently, will soon make you so strong in this direction that you will unconsciously, so to speak, be on your guard; in fact, the very moment that an adverse suggestion is given, your mind will spring up of its own accord with a wholesome suggestion to meet the requirements. To avoid becoming a victim to adverse suggestions — and we have such suggestions about us almost constantly — fill your mind so full of good, wholesome thoughts and suggestions that there is no room for anything else. Feel right at all times, and nothing from without can tempt you to think wrong. Make every good thought subconscious, and no adverse thought from without can possibly get into your subconscious mind at any time. A great many suggestions do not produce results, a fact which should be perfectly understood, because every thought that we think does contain some suggestion. When we are trying to impress good thoughts upon our minds, we want the good suggestions conveyed by those thoughts to take effect, but frequently they do not, and the reason is that a suggestion takes effect only when we exercise the power that is back of suggestion. The outward suggestion itself is simply the vehicle through which another power is acting, and that other power is nothing more nor less than the real life of that idea which the suggestion intends to convey.

April 19th

Ernest Holmes

We start a new enterprise and wonder what the chances of success are; have we realized that the outer is simply the inner manifested? When we go to a new place we shall find there only what we have taken with us. If we have taken success we will find success; if, on the other hand, we have taken failure we will find failure. This is the law; none can avoid it, none need try. Every living soul is a law unto his own life. "There is no law but my own soul shall set." Nothing can come upon the path of the soul but that thing that the soul attracts.

April 20th

Venice J. Bloodworth

The conscious mind is the supreme ruler in our mental world; it deals with all impressions of the visible world, gathered through the five senses; it carries the responsibility of decisions and is the gateway through which our destiny comes. Through the Magic Portal of conscious, creative, constructive thought, wisdom, knowledge, and understanding bring their richest gifts and place the scepter of power in your hand; while health, wealth, happiness and youth trail their glittering robes across the threshold of your consciousness and crystallize their royal attributes into your body and environment. But if the thoughts entertained by the conscious mind are hate, envy, anxiety, weakness, fear, or other negative thoughts, then the Magic Portal becomes the Iron Door of despair through which poverty, disease and unhappiness drag their ragged garments into your life.

April 21st

George Schubel

The "dark chamber" of a camera might with good reason be called the " illumining chamber" since it conditions the imaged object and shows it to the photographer as an object of light, wonderful to behold. Similarly when we enter our quiet darkened room and, by means of this room, into a place within our consciousness where all is quiet and subdued, we find ourselves peering within ourselves into what we might with good reason call the " illumining chamber " of the mind. It is in this state of objective consciousness in which reflection of the object of our thinking occurs; in which we meditate upon and contemplate our imaged thought; in which we are able to get our proper focus toward our thought; our proper perspective toward it, and in which we are able to consider it "in the right light." Somewhat later in our actual work we will give more attention to the manner in which our thought-image is brought into this illumined mental chamber, how it is there acted upon, and how it is subsequently developed. Suffice it here to say that the photographer would get a haphazard picture if he did not use this illumining chamber; if he did not peer carefully through it at the reflected object which he is planning to photograph. For the most part it would be ill-proportioned. Probably the light-image would be too dim or too sharp, or out of focus, and so it is in the matter of holding our thought-object in that place in our consciousness where it is subject to reflection; to meditation; to where we can get the proper " light upon it." If we do not see our thought-object by this means, it will be reproduced haphazardly as is now mostly the case in the spontaneous and undeliberated outward fulfillment of our inner desires. In the illumining chamber of our consciousness, we must review our projected thought; we must procure our proper perspective of it and we must judge there and then whether or not it is really worthwhile to bring forth into outward realization.

April 22nd

Prentice Mulford

We need to be careful of what we think and talk. Because thought runs in currents as real as those of air and water. Of what we think and talk we attract to us a like current of thought. This acts on mind or body for good or ill. If thought was visible to the physical eye we should see its currents flowing to and from people. We should see that persons similar in temperament, character and motive are in the same literal current of thought. We should see that the person in a despondent and angry mood was in the same current with others despondent or angry, and that each one in such moods serves as an additional battery or generator of such thought and is strengthening that particular current. We should see these forces working in similar manner and connecting the hopeful, courageous and cheerful, with all others hopeful, courageous and cheerful. When you are in low spirits or " blue " you have acting on you the thought current coming from all others in low spirits. You are in oneness with the despondent order of thought. The mind is then sick. It can be cured, but a permanent cure cannot always come immediately when one has long been in the habit of opening the mind to this current of thought. In attracting to us the current of any kind of evil, we become for a time one with evil. In the thought current of The Supreme Power for good we may become more and more as one with that power, or in Biblical phrase " One with God." That is the desirable thought current for us to attract.

April 23rd

Ernest Holmes

The highest attitude of mind, from which all else springs, is one of perfect calm and absolute trust in the Spirit. The one who can with perfect confidence look into the future and with perfect ease of mind rest in the present, and who never looks backward, but who has learned to be still in his own soul and wait upon the Spirit, he is the one who will the most completely demonstrate the supremacy of spiritual thought over all so-called material resistance. "Be still and know that I AM God."

April 24th

Joseph Murphy

The subconscious mind has the power to create; it also obeys the orders given to it by the conscious mind. Remember always this simple truth: The conscious mind has the power of choice; the subconscious does what it is told to do. The latter accepts your beliefs and convictions, and brings them into your experience. It is an infinite, creative power.

April 25th

Christian Larson

A most important fact, in connection with the great law, should be noted here. The creative power of the mind works more effectively, more intensely, and on a larger scale for that which is great, or wonderful, or deeply significant. It is a waste of time, therefore, to expect the small or the commonplace. We should entertain only great expectations. We thereby call forth a larger measure of creative power; and to apply an increased measure of this power, is to secure greater results, and in less time. The same rule should be observed elsewhere in this great work. Whatever we place in the mind, for creative power to work for, we should place the greatest and the most wonderful that we can feel, conceive or vision. To learn how to use this law, in the most effective manner, and for the greatest good — that is our purpose; but it is also well to state where this law should not be used. We should not permit this law to work with fear, worry, or other negatives. To entertain fear, is to place thoughts, pictures and impressions of fear deeply in the mind; and the creative power will work for those things. This power will work for anything that is placed deeply in the mind; and what this power continues to work for, will come to pass. That explains why our fears come upon us. If we could meet threatening situations, at any time, without placing thoughts of fear in the mind, the creative power within us would not work for those fears; and they would not come upon us. The same is true of all worries, anxieties, and other negatives. When we keep them out of the heart — deeper feeling — they will never amount to anything. To be able to do this, would mean incalculable gain, for fear is our worst enemy; and this thing we all can learn to do.

April 26th

Orison Swett Marden

The thing that Job held in his consciousness was the thing that came upon him. Joan of Arc saved her country, because from childhood she held the consciousness that she had been born to do that very thing. This poor unlettered peasant girl knew nothing about the great law of mental attraction, but unconsciously she worked with it. But for her consciousness of victory she never could have accomplished her stupendous work It is the victorious consciousness that achieves victory in every age and in every field. After many years' study of the lives and methods of successful men in every department of life, I have found that those who win out in a large way are great believers in themselves, in their power to succeed in the things they undertake. Great artists, scientists, inventors, explorers, generals, business men, and others, who have done the biggest things in their specialty, have always held the victorious consciousness. Success was the goal they constantly visualized, and they never wavered in their conviction that they would reach it. Men fail, not because of lack of ability, but because they do not hold the victorious consciousness, the success consciousness. They do not live in the expectancy of winning, in the belief that they will succeed in reaching the goal of their ambitions. They live rather in the expectation of possible failure, in fear of poverty, and coming to want, and they get what they hold in mind, what they habitually dwell upon. The pinched, narrow, limited, poverty-stricken, fear-filled consciousness; the consciousness that expects stingy returns, that expects poverty and does not believe it will get anything better, is responsible for more poverty than any other one thing.

April 27th

Ernest Holmes

We should more and more learn to think of things in the absolute, that is, to think of things as not limited by conditions. Realize at all times that the Spirit makes things out of Itself, and needs no beginning except its own self-recognition. Then we must cognize our relation to this great power as one of absolute correspondence; what we think into it, it takes up and does for us as we think. It should not be an effort so to think; we should do so with ease, without strain. The law must return to us; we have no responsibility except to provide the proper channel. It can return only in the exact way that we think. If we think struggle is the reality, we shall gain our demonstration, but struggle will have to be the result. There is a law of reflection between Mind and the one who thinks; and it is not only what a man thinks but also how he thinks that "shall be done unto him."

April 28th

Charles F. Haanel

The law is that thought will correlate with its object and bring forth in the material world the correspondence of the thing thought or produced in the mental world. We then discern the absolute necessity of seeing that every thought has the inherent germ of truth in order that the law of growth will bring into manifestation good, for good alone can confer any permanent power. The principle which gives the thought the dynamic power to correlate with its object, and therefore to master every adverse human experience, is the law of attraction, which is another name for love. This is an eternal and fundamental principle, inherent in all things, in every system of Philosophy, in every Religion, and in every Science. There is no getting away from the law of love. It is feeling that imparts vitality to thought. Feeling is desire, and desire is love. Thought impregnated with love becomes invincible. We find this truth emphasized wherever the power of thought is understood, The Universal Mind is not only Intelligence, but it is substance, and this substance is the attractive force which brings electrons together by the law of attraction so that they form atoms; the atoms in turn are brought together by the same law and form molecules; molecules take objective forms; and so we find that the law of love is the creative force behind every manifestation, not only of atoms, but of worlds, of the Universe, of everything of which the imagination can form any conception.

April 29th

Jeanie P. Owens

You may perhaps say that we cannot control our thoughts, that we cannot prevent our minds dwelling upon certain subjects even against our desire. I say most emphatically that we can, and, if we are in earnest in the matter, we will. "For every man there is a kingdom over which he is born to have absolute sway — the Kingdom of his Thoughts, his realm of mentality. Few of us realize this sufficiently to take upon ourselves the true dignity of our kingship." Of course if we are not in earnest we will continue simply to drift with the stream of our wayward fancy, and must take the consequences. It is true that we cannot prevent certain ideas coming into our minds, but we can prevent them staying there; we can drive them out again, though it should at first be twenty times an hour or oftener. An old divine, writing on this subject, says, "We cannot prevent foul birds of the air flying over our heads, but we can prevent them building nests in our hair." If we resolutely determine that we will not allow our minds to be possessed by certain thoughts, and whenever they recur, deliberately and by an effort of will put them from us by turning our minds in another direction, by-and-by, like visitors who find themselves always unwelcome, they will gradually cease to trouble us, and finally will depart altogether. I am not referring here only to thoughts which are wrong in themselves, but to all anxious, morbid, or even unpleasant thoughts which worry and annoy us through their persistency; they are all part of the same poisonous brood against which we have to wage unremitting war, and which, if we would be healthy as well as happy, we must cast out of our minds completely.

April 30th

Henry Thomas Hamblin

The Unseen is greater than the Seen, therefore to work in the Unseen is to deal with the "cause" of which the outward life is the "effect." By working in the Unseen by means of meditation, affirmation, visualizing and by holding in our mind the highest ideals we arouse the Power that lies hidden within us. The Power that is within us is the power of the Universal Mind or Spirit, therefore it is infinite and illimitable; the only limit there can be is the limitation we place upon it by our lack of faith. Therefore in all your difficulties and battles remember that the Power within you is infinite. You are one with the Infinite if you will only believe it, if you can only realize it. Rise up and go forward with confidence, your highest ideals can. be attained too, if you will believe and have faith and reach upward to higher and better things. I affirm for you the inward knowledge of these things.

May

May 1st

Ernest Holmes

In the Infinity of mind, which is the principle of all metaphysics and of all life, there is nothing but mind, and that which mind does. That is all there is in the Universe. That is all there ever was or ever will be. This mind is acted upon by our thought, and so our thought becomes the law of our lives. It is just as much a law in our individual lives as God's thought is in the larger life of the Universe. For the sake of clearness, think of yourself as in this Mind, think of yourself as a center in it. That is your principle. You think, and Mind produces the thing. One of the big points to remember is that we do not have to create; all that we have to do is to think. Mind, the only Mind that there is, creates.

May 2nd

Christian Larson

To define scientific thinking, it may be stated that your thinking is scientific when your thought has a direct tendency to produce what you want, or when all the forces of your mind are working together for the purpose you desire to fulfill. Your thinking is unscientific when your thought has a tendency to produce what is detrimental, or when your mental forces are working against you. To think scientifically, the first essential is to think only such thoughts and permit only such mental attitudes as you know to be in your favor; and the second essential is to make only such thoughts subjective. In other words, every thought should be right and every thought should be a force. When every thought is scientific, it will be right, and when every thought is subjective it will be a force. Positively refuse to think of what you do not wish to retain or experience. Think only of what you desire, and expect only what you desire, even when the very contrary seems to be coming into your life. Make it a point to have definite results in mind at all times. Permit no thinking to be aimless. Every aimless thought is time and energy wasted, while every thought that is inspired with a definite aim will help to realize that aim, and if all your thoughts are inspired with a definite aim, the whole power of your mind will be for you and will work with you in realizing what you have in view. That you should succeed is therefore assured, because there is enough power in your mind to realize your ambitions, provided all of that power is used in working for your ambitions. And in scientific thinking all the power of mind and thought is being caused to work directly and constantly for what you wish to attain and achieve.

May 3rd

Joseph Murphy

Jesus said, "For ye have the poor always with you; but me ye have not always." The poor states of consciousness are always with us in this sense, that no matter how much wealth you now have, there is something you want with all your heart. It may be a problem of health; perhaps a son or daughter needs guidance, or harmony is lacking in the home. At that moment you are poor. We could not know what abundance was, except we were conscious of lack. "I have chosen twelve, and one you of is a devil." Whether it be the king of England or the boy in the slums, we are all born into limitation and into the race belief. It is through these limitations we grow. We could never discover the Inner Power, except through problems and difficulties; these are our poor states which prod us in seeking the solution. We could not know what joy was, except we could shed a tear of sorrow. We must be aware of poverty, to seek liberation and freedom, and ascend into God's opulence.

May 4th

James Allen

Men, like schoolboys, find themselves in standards or classes to which their ignorance or knowledge entitles them. The curriculum of the sixth standard is a mystery to the boy in the first; it is outside and beyond the circle of his comprehension; but he reaches it by persistent effort and patient growth in learning. By mastering and outgrowing all the standards between, he comes at last to the sixth, and makes its learning his own; and beyond still is the sphere of the teacher. So in life, men whose deeds are dark and selfish, full of passion and personal desire, cannot comprehend those whose deeds are bright and unselfish, whose minds are calm, deep, and pure, but they can reach this higher standard, this enlarged consciousness, by effort in right doing, by growth in thought and moral comprehension. And above and beyond all lower and higher standards stand the Teachers of mankind, the Cosmic Masters, the Saviours of the world whom the adherents of the various religions worship. There are grades in teachers as in pupils, and some there are who have not yet reached the rank and position of Master, yet, by the sterling morality of their character, are guides and teachers; but to occupy a pulpit or rostrum does not make a man a teacher. A man is constituted a teacher by virtue of that moral greatness which calls forth the respect and reverence of mankind.

May 5th

Ernest Holmes

Man lives in a mind that presses in upon him from all sides with infinite possibilities, with infinite creative power. The divine urge of infinite love crowds itself upon him, and awaits his recognition. Being the image of this Power, his thought also must be the Word or cause in the life. At the center of his being is all the power that he will need on the path of his unfoldment; all the mind that man has is as much of this Infinite Mind as he allows to flow through him. We have often thought of God as far off, and of man as a being separate from the All Good; now we are coming to see that God and man are one, and that that One is simply awaiting man's recognition, that he may spring into being and become to man all that he could wish or want. "As the father has inherent life in himself, so hath he given to the Son to have life within himself." It could not be otherwise; we are all in Mind and Mind is always creating for us as we think; and as we are thinking creatures, always thinking, our happiness depends upon our thought.

May 6th

Robert Collier

Do you want a situation? Close your eyes and realize that somewhere is the position for which you of all people are best fitted, and which is best fitted to your ability. The position where you can do the utmost of good, and where life, in turn, offers the most to you. Realize that Universal Mind knows exactly where this position is, and that through your subconscious mind you, too, can know it. Realize that this is YOUR position, that it NEEDS you, that it belongs to you, that it is right for you to have it, that you are entitled to it. Hold this thought in mind every night for just a moment, then go to sleep knowing that your subconscious mind HAS the necessary information as to where this position is and how to get in touch with it. Mind you — not WILL have, but HAS. The earnest realization of this will bring that position to you, and you to it, as surely as the morrow will bring the sun. Make the law of supply operative and you find that the things you seek are seeking you. Get firmly fixed in your own mind the definite conviction that you can do anything you greatly want to do. There is no such thing as lack of opportunity. There is no such thing as only one opportunity. You are subject to a law of boundless and perpetual opportunity, and you can enforce that law in your behalf just as widely as you need. Opportunity is infinite and ever present.

May 7th

Uriel Buchanan

There is no limit to the possibilities of the human mind when once freed from the influence of race beliefs and erroneous thoughts. At times when you feel this unlimited power of the mind and will, when you know that there is something within which gives you the power to overcome every influence of adversity, if you will encourage this mood and maintain it permanently, you will increase the drawing force of the mind and will attract to you the association and environment corresponding to your highest ideals. We must grow into a faith in the existence of the Supreme Force and our ability to draw to us an unlimited supply for every purpose and demand. It will come to us and give an increase of strength and inspiration in all effort, all progress, as we learn to keep the mind in the right attitude of faith in the reality of this power and „maintain the earnest desire to receive it. Attracting force from the unseen makes all work a pleasure. We feel our nearness to the source of all things, and know that nothing can take from us its help and protection.

May 8th

Christian Larson

It is the meek that inherit the earth, because such minds have the greatest creative power. What we create, we inherit; no more, no less. Therefore, when we gain the power to create much, we shall inherit much. To meet everything in the attitude of harmony is of the highest importance, because whatever we enter into harmony with, while in a state of aspiration, that we meet on the superior side. The qualities that we enter into mental contact with, we absorb; therefore, it is a great advantage to mentally meet the superior only. When we constantly aspire, and live in harmony with everything, we enter into true relationship with the better qualities that are latent in every person or condition with which we come in contact; and consequently permit the superior things in life to impress our minds at every turn. And the value of having only superior impressions in mind is so great that it cannot be calculated. Superior impressions originate superior thoughts; and as man is as he thinks, superior thoughts will develop superiority in him. And the superior man creates a superior fate, a better future and a more wonderful destiny. By entering into harmony with all things, and by constantly dwelling in the aspiring attitude, you absorb the good qualities from your enemies and your adversaries. And since evil is only the good perverted, when you take the good out of anything, there is nothing left to be perverted; consequently there can exist no more enmity nor adversity in that place. Absorb the good power that is back of adversity, and adversity ceases to be. In this way, we can truthfully say,

"We have met the enemy, and they are ours," because the very life of that which was against us has been appropriated by ourselves and engaged to work for our interest and promotion.

May 9th

Ernest Holmes

Cause and effect must obtain everywhere. Do not even fuss about your Karma; too often we hear people say, "This is my Karma." This may be true enough, but how many people know what they mean when they use the word Karma? Do you realize that your Karma is nothing but your false thinking, and that the only way to escape it is to think the truth, and that brings in the higher law? When the greater comes in the lesser leaves because there is no longer anything to give life to it. The past is gone when we learn to forgive and to forget.

May 10th

Venice J. Bloodworth

Everything is first worked out in the unseen, before it is visible in the seen; in the ideal before it shows forth in the real; in the spiritual before it manifests in the material. Your subconscious mind is bringing you the matured fruits of your mental action, so let's get busy and build something worthy of the latent powers within you. Your imagination is a divine gift, for with mental images you may build any condition you desire. First comes the idea, then a mental picture of that idea; these are the thought seeds that the subconscious mind uses to grow our conditions and environment. All possessions depend on consciousness. Do you want a home? Then build it in your imagination. It must be in your mind before it will ever be anywhere else. Don't stop to count the cost. You are not limited as to material; you are drawing on the inexhaustible Universal Supply. Build your house, fill in the details, furnish it after your heart's desire

May 11th

Joseph Murphy

Prayer is like a captain directing the course of his ship. You must have a destination. You must know where you are going. The captain of the ship, knowing the laws of navigation, regulates his course accordingly. If the ship is turned from its course by storms or unruly waves, he calmly redirects it along its true course. You are the captain on the bridge, and you are giving the orders in the way of thoughts, feelings, opinions, beliefs, moods, and mental tones. Keep your eye on the beam. You go where your vision is! Cease, therefore, looking at all the obstacles, delays, and impediments that would cause you to go off your course. Be definite and positive. Decide where you are going. Know that your mental attitude is the ship which will take you from the mood of lack and limitation, to the mood and feeling of opulence, and to the belief in the inevitable law of God working for you.

May 12th

Charles F. Haanel

Thought is a spiritual activity and is therefore creative, but make no mistake, thought will create nothing unless it is consciously, systematically, and constructively directed; and herein is the difference between idle thinking, which is simply a dissipation of effort, and constructive thinking, which means practically unlimited achievement. We have found that everything we get comes to us by the Law of Attraction. A happy thought cannot exist in an unhappy consciousness; therefore the consciousness must change, and, as the consciousness changes, all conditions necessary to meet the changed consciousness must gradually change, in order to meet the requirements of the new situation. In creating a Mental Image or an Ideal, we are projecting a thought into the Universal Substance from which all things are created. This Universal Substance is Omnipresent, Omnipotent and Omniscient. Are we to inform the Omniscient as to the proper channel to be used to materialize our demand? Can the finite advise the Infinite? This is the cause of failure; of every failure. We recognize the Omnipresence of the Universal Substance, but we fail to appreciate the fact that this substance is not only Omnipresent, but is Omnipotent and Omniscient, and consequently will set causes in motion concerning which we may be entirely ignorant. We can best conserve our interests by recognizing the Infinite Power and Infinite Wisdom of the Universal Mind, and in this way become a channel whereby the Infinite can bring about the realization of our desire. This means that recognition brings about realization, therefore make use of the principle, recognize the fact that you are a part of the whole, and that a part must be the same in kind and quality as the whole; the only difference there can possibly by, is in degree. When this tremendous fact begins to permeate your consciousness, when you really come into a realization of the fact that you (not your body, but the Ego), the "I," the spirit which thinks is an integral part of the great whole, that it is the same in substance, in quality, in kind, that the Creator could create nothing different from Himself, you will also be able to say, "The Father and I are one" and you will come into an understanding of the beauty, the grandeur, the transcendental opportunities which have been placed at your disposal.

May 13th

Ernest Holmes

Life is for us today. There will be no change for tomorrow unless we do the changing today. Today we are setting in motion the power of tomorrow. Today is God's day, and we must extract from it what of life we are to live. Tomorrow in the divine course of events will care for itself. The soul that learns to live in the great gladness of today will never weary of life but will find that he is living in an eternal here and now. Now, all good is his; now, all life, truth and love are his; now, he has entered in, and the good things of life are his today.

May 14th

Christian Larson

When man discovers the state of self-supremacy, he can no longer believe in the control of environment as a principle; and is therefore compelled to declare that the control of environment is no longer true to him. And, as he is permitted to speak only for himself, and judge only his own life, he must refuse absolutely to believe in the control of environment under any condition whatever. To believe that others are controlled by environment, is to judge where he has no authority, and also to place himself once again in the belief that environment controls man. To place himself in that belief is to enter the attitude of self-submission, and submit himself to the influence of everything that enters his sphere of existence. It is therefore evident that the principal reason why those who know of self-supremacy do not master fate, is because they are not true to their own convictions. They believe that the principle of self-supremacy exists, but they also believe that the control of environment exists. They try to believe both to be true at the same time, which is impossible. If the one exists as a living power in the life of a person, the other does not exist in the life of that person. It would be just as reasonable to believe that light and darkness could exist in the same place at the same time. To try to believe in the idea of self-supremacy and the control of environment at the same time, is to live in confusion; and he who lives in confusion controls practically nothing. He is therefore more or less controlled by everything. When man is convinced that he is, in himself, master over his life, he can no longer believe that his life is controlled by environment. He must absolutely reject the latter belief; both cannot be true to anyone mind; therefore, every mind must decide which one of these beliefs to accept as absolutely true, and which one to reject as absolutely untrue.

The Within Creates The Without: Daily Meditations

May 15th

Prentice Mulford

The material mind does not regard its thought as an actual element as real as air or water. The spiritual mind knows that everyone of its thousand daily secret thoughts are real things, acting on the minds of the persons they are sent to. The spiritual mind knows that matter or the material is only an expression of spirit or force; that such matter is ever changing in accordance with the spirit that makes or externalizes itself in the form we call matter, and therefore, if the thought of health, strength and recuperation is constantly held to in the mind, such thought of health, strength and rejuvenation will express itself in the body, making maturity never ceasing, vigor never ending, and the keenness of every physical sense ever increasing. The material mind thinks matter, or what is known by our physical senses to be the largest part of what exists. The spiritual mind regards matter as the coarser or cruder expression of spirit and the smallest part of what really exists. The material mind is made sad at the contemplation of decay. The spiritual mind attaches little importance to decay, knowing in such decay that spirit or the moving force in all things is simply taking the dead body or the rotten tree to pieces, and that it will build them up again as before temporarily into some other new physical form of life and beauty. The mind of the body thinks that its physical senses of seeing, hearing and feeling constitute all the senses you possess. The higher mind or mind of the spirit knows that it possesses other senses akin to those of physical sight and hearing, but more powerful and far reaching.

May 16th

James Allen

The body is the servant of the mind. It obeys the operations of the mind, whether they be deliberately chosen or automatically expressed. At the bidding of unlawful thoughts the body sinks rapidly into disease and decay; at the command of glad and beautiful thoughts it becomes clothed with youthfulness and beauty. Disease and health, like circumstances, are rooted in thought. Sickly thoughts will express themselves through a sickly body. Thoughts of fear have been known to kill a man as speedily as a bullet, and they are continually killing thousands of people just as surely though less rapidly. The people who live in fear of disease are the people who get it. Anxiety quickly demoralizes the whole body, and lays it open to the entrance of disease; while impure thoughts, even if not physically indulged, will soon shatter the nervous system. Strong, pure, and happy thoughts build up the body in vigor and grace. The body is a delicate and plastic instrument, which responds readily to the thoughts by which it is impressed, and habits of thought will produce their own effects, good or bad, upon it.

May 17th

Ernest Holmes

We have a right to have and should expect to have in this world all that will make for the comfort and for the luxuries of life. What matter how much we have, if we rob no other soul to get it? Shall not the Power that so lavishly spreads Itself out into nature give to us Its highest expression, all that we can ask? We dishonor God when we claim less than all. Until we can expand our thought so that we shall be able to say also, "I AM," we need not expect to get great results.

May 18th

Orison Swett Marden

There is a power in man, back of the flesh, but not of it, working in harmony with the Divine Intelligence in the great cosmic ocean of energy, of limitless supply, that is, today, performing miracles in invention, in agriculture, in commerce, in industry. This power, which is creative and everywhere operative, is destined to lift every created thing up to the peak of its possibilities. It is latent in you, awaiting expression, awaiting your cooperation to realize your ambition. The first step toward utilizing it is to visualize the ideal of what you want to make real, the ideal of the man or the woman you aim to be, and the things you want to do. Without this initial step the further process of creating is impossible. No matter what happens, always hold fast to the thought that you can be what you long to be; that you can do the thing you want to do, and picture yourself always as succeeding in what you desire to come true in your life. No matter how urgent duties or obligations may for a time hold you back, how circumstances and conditions may contradict the possibility of your success; how people, even your own people, may blame or misunderstand you, may even call you a crank, crazy, a conceited egotist, hold fast to your faith in your dream, in yourself. Cling to your vision, nurse it, for it is the God-inspired model by which He is urging you to shape your life.

May 19th

Joseph Murphy

There is a subconscious mind within you; you should learn how to use it in the same manner as a man learns to use electricity. Man controls electricity with wires, tubes, and bulbs, plus his knowledge of the laws of conductivity and insulation, etc. We must learn about the tremendous power and the intelligence within us, and use it wisely. Many men are beginning to realize the true importance of the subconscious mind. In business many men are using it to achieve success and promotion. Edison, Ford, Marconi, Einstein, and many others have used the subconscious mind; it has given to them the insight and the "know how" for all of their great achievements in science, industry, and art. Research has shown that the ability to bring into action the subconscious powers has determined the success of all of the great scientific and research workers. There is a tremendous dynamo within you, and you can use it. You can also be completely released from tension and frustration. You can discover the abundant energy within you enabling you to energize and vitalize all parts of your body.

May 20th

Christian Larson

When your plans cannot be carried through at present, do not feel downcast or discouraged. Just be glad. Give gladness to your mind and you give clearness to your mind; and a clear mind can see how to evolve better plans. When your dreams do not come true and your ideals do not become real, refuse to be sad or disconsolate. Instead, rejoice with great joy to know that you are greater than your dreams, and wholly sufficient unto yourself regardless of what may transpire in the real or the ideal. Thus you will give expression to that greater power within you which surely can make your ideals real and make all your dreams come true. Prove that your cherished dreams are not necessary to your happiness, and all of those dreams will come true. Prove that you do not need the things you want, and you will get them, provided of course that you give all that is in you to the life you live. Prove that you already are sufficient in yourself, and have sufficient in the richness of your own world, and more and more will gather for you, both in the within and in the without. It is much gathering more; much in the within gathering more everywhere; it is your own strength inspiring all things to come with strength; it is the spirit of the great life aroused in yourself causing all things of greatness and worth to come and gather in the entire world of your own life. And it is in this spirit that we live and move and have our being, when the soul continues to sing that sweet reassuring refrain just be glad.

May 21st

Ernest Holmes

In the center of your own soul choose what you want to become, to accomplish; keep it to yourself. Every day in the silence of absolute conviction know that it is now done. It is just as much done, as far as you are concerned, as it will be when you experience it in the outer. Imagine yourself to be what you want to be. See only that which you desire, refuse even to think of the other. Stick to it, never doubt. Say many times a day, "I AM that thing," realize what this means. It means that the great Universal power of Mind is that, and it cannot fail.

May 22nd

Uriel Buchanan

Thought is an invisible substance which acts apart from the body. It vibrates through space and exerts an influence over responsive minds. As you learn how to make the best use of thought, how to concentrate and direct it, you can accomplish more in any business or undertaking and attract more and more of the element of power which gives success. The mind is like a magnet. It attracts an element of force corresponding in nature to the dominating quality of thought. If you hold in your mind the positive thought of determination, enthusiasm, cheerfulness, strength, sympathy, hope and courage, you will attract more and more of such qualities from the unseen realm of mind. To set your thoughts in the right direction of desire and aspiration for these and similar elements of success you will send out invisible waves which will act on others whose thoughts will meet and mingle with your own, you will gather new strength from such contact and will attract forces favorable to the attainment of your purpose. But if you are under the influence of fear, of discouragement or hopelessness, you will attract thoughts of like kind which will affect you disagreeably. Association with any one of lower thought will cause you to absorb his thought. Though you may be positive and determined, you will be influenced more or less by whatever quality of thought dominates the mind of your associate. You will carry a part of his negative, discordant thought with you and will send out a similar influence which others will feel. Thought is the moving force of all progress or retrogression, of all success or failure. The nature of the thought we hold determines the conditions which surround us. Like creates like in the domain of mind, and there is a force within us which is ever at work to create a material correspondence of every persistent desire.

May 23rd

Robert Collier

The subconscious mind does not reason inductively. It takes the thoughts you send in to it and works them out to their logical conclusion. Send to it thoughts of health and strength, and it will work out health and strength in your body. Let suggestions of disease, fear of sickness or accident, penetrate to it, either through your own thoughts or the talk of those around you, and you are very likely to see the manifestation of disease working out in yourself. Your mind is master of your body. It directs and controls every function of your body. Your body is in effect a little universe in itself, and mind is its radiating center — the sun which gives light and life to all your system, and around which the whole revolves. And your conscious thought is master of this sun center. As Emile Coué puts it — "The conscious can put the subconscious mind over the hurdles."

May 24th

Venice J. Bloodworth

The difference in men is almost wholly due to the difference in their thoughts. Therefore, you can readily see that to have health you must concentrate on health; to be loved you must love your brother; to have abundance of material wealth you must think abundance. That is the law and no permanent good was ever acquired in any other way. If you lay a lot of steel shavings on a barrel, every time someone jars the barrel some of the shavings will fall off; but put a magnet under them and you may turn the barrel upside down and the shavings will stick. So it is with human beings; Whatever You have made yourself a magnet for you will get.

May 25th

Ernest Holmes

Whatever we discover to be true about God I am at the same time realizing to be a truth about myself. Whatever I find to be a truth about myself, expanding my consciousness, I realize that it is a universal truth. Herein is the mystery of life. You and I are intelligent centers using the creative word for that which we will constructively or destructively, and that creative word which we use becomes the law unto the thing whereunto it is sent and becomes the concept behind it and projects the thing, creates the thing in our life. And so it might be said of my life that I AM the word and without the word is not anything made into my life that is made, and the word was with me and the word was me. Absolutely everything in my life. That is a new way of looking at life, but it is absolute truth. We cannot help it; we cannot get away from it. Moreover, without my word nothing is made in my life and all things that are in my life were made by my word whether I know it or not. Because of that very fact therein lies your very divinity, and otherwise you would not be divine. You can be mechanical like a blade of grass. But we have been given the ability to choose the word we speak, and therein lies our very limitation. It is simply the misuse of our divine nature, the abuse of it, the lack of knowing that our word is cause, the ignorance that has caused us to speak a negative word. And because the word is the concept and the concept is the thing and the thing is the word itself, that word has created a negative condition. To change that negative condition I have got to use a different word, but the same cause, intelligence, and speak my word.

May 26th

Christian Larson

When you sympathize naturally and constantly with the superior side of people, all the desires of mind will gradually fix their attention upon the superior; and when all the desires of mind desire the superior you will be irresistibly drawn into superior association. And nothing, not even old abnormal sympathies can keep you away from your own. When you sympathize with the greater possibilities in things, your attention will be constantly turned upon the greater; your mind will be more and more impressed with the greater, until every thought becomes a power for greatness; and with this power you will move into greatness, regardless of any obstacle that may appear in the way. The power of sympathy is one of the greatest powers of attraction in existence; therefore, when we sympathize only with the superior, we will be drawn into superiority, and this will steadily change our environments for the better. Thus, by producing a change in the mental world, we can revolutionize the external world. When life is viewed comprehensively, it becomes very evident that the actions of the person determine what the external conditions and circumstances of that person are to be; but every personal action is caused by a mental action; therefore, the change of environment must be preceded by a change of mind. To master thought is to master fate; but thought cannot be mastered until mind acts exclusively upon the principle that man is inherently complete master over his entire domain. The strongest evidence that can be produced in favor of the statement that man's circumstances are caused by the active elements of his mental world, is that of creative ability, because it is being demonstrated every day that the man with a strong creative mind has destiny at his feet. Creative ability can absolutely change all circumstances; but it is not an external power; it is simply an active element in mind.

May 27th

Henry Thomas Hamblin

There is the conscious mind and there is the subconscious mind. The conscious mind gathers knowledge and experience through the senses. It learns from books, conversation and experience. It reasons and forms conclusions. Finally its thoughts pass down into the subconscious mind. The subconscious mind is the mind of action. It is responsible for all that we do. It is the seat of memory and of instinct. It is a reservoir of tremendous power, it is of extraordinary intelligence, it carries out all the complicated processes within the body, which make life possible. The wisest and most learned of men cannot begin to fathom its wonderful powers, but in spite of this we know enough about its manner of working to enable us to control it, and by controlling it, we control our actions, and by controlling our actions we shape our life, and overcome what is called fate. The subconscious mind, although so wonderfully intelligent and possessed of such extraordinary powers, acts entirely upon suggestion. That is to say, it follows blindly and faithfully the thoughts that are sent down into it. Therefore upon our thoughts depends what sort of actions are brought forth. If evil thoughts are sent down into the subconscious mind, then evil, destructive action will be the natural result. If thoughts of weakness and failure are entertained, then weak actions leading to failure will inevitably follow. On the other hand, if good thoughts are entertained, then constructive good action will result, and if strong, successful thoughts are entertained, they bring forth robust, constructive action, which leads to success and achievement.

May 28th

Joseph Murphy

You are familiar with this fundamental fact: When money is circulated freely in a country, its financial condition is healthy. Let there be a healthy circulation of money in your life also, particularly in your mental attitude. Believe that money is good; think of all of the good you can do with it. Become a mental inlet and outlet for a constant stream of wealth forever flowing to you and forever flowing from you in a perfect circulation. If you are having financial difficulties, trying to make ends meet, it means you have not convinced your subconscious mind that you will always have plenty and some to spare. You know men and women who work a few hours a week, and make fabulous sums of money. They do not strive or slave hard. Do not believe the story that the only way you can become wealthy or successful is by the sweat of your brow and hard labor. It is not so; the effortless way of life is the best. Do the thing you love to do, and do it for the joy and thrill of it. Sing at your work; you will, if you love it; also, if you love your work, you are bound to be a success.

May 29th

Ernest Holmes

All things come to us through the use of our thought. If we have a small concept of life we will always be doing small things. First in the creative series is the Word, but the Word carries us no further than our consciousness back of it. Unless we are constantly expanding our thought we are not growing. Growth is the law of life and it is necessary. We cannot stand still. If you want to do a new thing, get a new thought and then you will have the power of attraction which has the possibility of drawing to you the circumstances which will make for the fulfillment of your desires. Get over the old idea of limitation.

May 30th

Walter C. Lanyon

"The Spirit of the Consciousness of the Presence of God is the source of all supply.' Not of SOME supply, but of all supply. When you know this, you will not try to hoard there will be no need, for supply will be as much present in one locality as another. It will be wherever you are and wherever you desire it. Do you hear? You who read this page? Look between the lines; I speak to you. I cast not my pearls before swine, but I AM pouring them out to you. I AM giving you the keys to the gates of heaven, which you have sought through many avenues, and not yet found. The sordid robes of personality, name, and fame will fall finally from you, and you shall put on the glorious shimmering robes of immortality. I speak to you. Do you hear? You who read this page? When you are ready to lay down your life, then shall you find it. Then you shall find that you are alive for the first time, and, instead of the ghastly futility of trying to get enough health, happiness, and supply to live by, you will find yourself in the Presence of the All, there nothing is lacking.

May 31st

Orison Swett Marden

One reason why most of us do such little, unoriginal things is because we do not sufficiently nurse our visions and longings. The plan of the building must come before the building. We climb by the ladder of our visions, our dreams. The sculptor's model must live in his own mind before he can call it out of the marble. We do not half realize the mental force we generate by persistently visualizing our ideal, by the perpetual clinging to our dreams, the vision of the thing we long to do or to be. We do not know that nursing our desires makes the mental pictures sharper, more clean cut, and that these mental processes are completing the plans of our future life building, filling in the outlines and details, and drawing to us out of the invisible energy of the universe the materials for our actual building. There is no other one thing you will find so helpful in the attainment of your ambition as the habit of visualizing what you are trying to accomplish, visualizing it vividly, just as distinctly, just as vigorously as possible, because this makes a magnet of the mind to attract what one is after. All about us we see young men focusing their minds with intensity and persistence on their special aims and attracting to themselves marvelous results. A medical student holds in his mind a vision of himself as a great physician or surgeon, and in a few years we are amazed at the size of his practice. He called it out of the great universal supply by his perpetual visualizing, the constant intensifying of his desire, and the unceasing struggle on the material plan to make his dream come true.

June

The Within Creates The Without: Daily Meditations

June 1st

Christian Larson

A great many men and women, after discovering the immense power of mind, have come to the conclusion that they might change circumstances by exercising mental power upon those circumstances in some mysterious manner, but such a practice means nothing but a waste of energy. The way to control circumstances is to control the forces within yourself to make a greater human being of yourself, and as you become greater and more competent, you will naturally gravitate into better circumstances. In this connection, we should remember that like attracts like. If you want that which is better, make yourself better. If you want to realize the ideal, make yourself more ideal. If you want better friends, make yourself a better friend. If you want to associate with people of worth, make yourself more worthy. If you want to meet that which is agreeable, make yourself more agreeable. If you want to enter conditions and circumstances that are more pleasing, make yourself more pleasing. In brief, whatever you want, produce that something in yourself, and you will positively gravitate towards the corresponding conditions in the external world. But to improve yourself along those lines, it is necessary to apply for that purpose, all the power you possess. You cannot afford to waste any of it, and every misuse of the mind will waste power. Avoid all destructive attitudes of the mind, such an anger, hatred, malice, envy, jealousy, revenge, depression, discouragement, disappointment, worry, fear, and so on. Never antagonize, never resist what is wrong, and never try to get even. Make the best use of your own talent and the best that is in store for you will positively come your way. When others seem to take advantage of you, do not retaliate by trying to take advantage of them. Use your power in improving yourself, so that you can do better and better work. That is how you are going to win in the race.

June 2nd

Ernest Holmes

How can we enter in, if at one and the same time we are believing for ourselves and beholding the beam in our brother's eye? Does that not obstruct the view and pervert our own natures? We must see only the good and let nothing else enter into our minds. Universal love to all people and to all things is but returning love to the source of all love, to Him who creates all in love and holds all in divine care. The sun shines on all alike. Shall we separate and divide where God has so carefully united? We are dividing our own things when we do this, and sooner or later the Law of Absolute Justice that weighs out to each one his just measure will balance the account, and then we shall be obliged to suffer for the mistakes we have made. God does not bring this agony on us but we have imposed it on ourselves. If from selfish motives alone, we must love all things and look upon all things as good, made from the substance of the Father.

June 3rd

Joseph Murphy

Look around you wherever you live and you will notice that the vast majority of mankind lives in the world without; the more enlightened men are intensely interested in the world within. Remember, it is the world within, namely, your thoughts, feelings, and imagery that makes your world without. It is, therefore, the only creative power, and everything, which you find in your world of expression, has been created by you in the inner world of your mind consciously or unconsciously.

June 4th

Robert Collier

The men who have made their mark in this world all had one trait in common — they believed in themselves! "But," you may say, "how can I believe in myself when I have never yet done anything worthwhile, when everything I put my hand to seems to fail?" You can't, of course. That is, you couldn't if you had to depend upon your conscious mind alone. But just remember what one far greater than you said — "I can of mine own self do nothing. The Father that is within me — He doeth the works." That same "Father" is within you. And it is by knowing that He is in you, and that through Him you can do anything that is right, that you can acquire that belief in yourself which is so necessary. Certainly the Mind that imaged the heavens and the earth and all that they contain has all wisdom, all power, all abundance. With this Mind to call upon, you know there is no problem too difficult for you to undertake. The knowing of this is the first step. Faith. But St. James tells us — "Faith without works is dead." So go on to the next step. Decide on the one thing you want most from life. No matter what it may be. There is no limit, you know, to Mind. Visualize this thing that you want. See it, feel it, BELIEVE in it. Make your mental blueprint, and begin to build!

June 5th

James Allen

Man is buffeted by circumstances so long as he believes himself to be the creature of outside conditions. But when he realizes that he may command the hidden soil and seeds of his being out of which circumstances grow, he then becomes the rightful master of himself. That circumstances grow out of thought every man knows who has for any length of time practiced self-control and self-purification, for he will have noticed that the alteration in his circumstances has been in exact ratio with his altered mental condition. So true is this that when a man earnestly applies himself to remedy the defects in his character, and makes swift and marked progress, he passes rapidly through a succession of vicissitudes.

June 6th

Ernest Holmes

Since all is Mind and the only activity of Mind is thought, and the only thing you get out of Mind is what you first think into it, what you think is of the greatest importance. How you think it, the bigness with which you think it: If you could only conceive a very small thing, that is all you would physically get. Here we realize that we are not dealing with anything that is physical. There is no physical explanation for anything on earth or anything else and there never will be. All manifestation is backed up by a definite idea. Every idea is a thought in your life and mind and everything that happens to us is backed up by some mental attitude. We have on the one hand all Mind, or the substance which forms itself around our thought; on the other hand, we have the thought around which it forms. And here is something you must never forget: that Life can only operate for us by flowing through us, never in any other way. You will never demonstrate until behind your mental attitude is the belief that you have received before you have received that thing which is sought. And if you will study the life of any successful businesspeople, they are doing the same thing unconsciously. All we are doing is learning to take the same thing and systematically apply it for definite purposes, and it operates.

June 7th

Christian Larson

When you meet reverses, just be glad; for do we not again remember how soon a smile of God can change the world? It is not gloom that dispels darkness; it is not disconsolance that makes the mind brilliant and the soul strong. But if we would turn the tide of ill fortune we need all our brilliancy and all our strength. To master fate, to conquer destiny, to make life our own, we must be all there is in us to be. Then we must remember that it is sunshine that makes the flowers grow, and that transforms the acorn into a great and massive oak. Everything in nature, and in man, the crowning glory of nature, responds with pleasure to the magic touch of the smiling sunbeam. For again we must remember that all things respond to the call of rejoicing; all things gather where life is a song. Promise yourself that whatever may come you will always remember just be glad. When good things come into life, gladness will make them better. When things come that should not have come, gladness will so brighten your mind that you can see clearly how to turn everything to good account. Whatever happens or not, just be glad, and it will be much better than it possibly could have been otherwise. Therefore, gladness is not a mere sentiment. It pays. It is not a luxury for the favored few alone. It is a necessity that all should secure in abundance.

June 8th

Prentice Mulford

Your every thought is a force, as real as a current of electricity is a force. The thoughts you are now putting out are now working to shape your face and body, affecting your health for good or ill, and making or losing for you money. If you think poverty, you put out an actual force to attract poverty. If in mind you are always seeing yourself growing poorer and poorer, if at every venture you fear and teach yourself to expect to lose money, if your heart quakes every time you pull out your purse, you are by an inevitable force in nature, or spiritual law, attracting poverty. Your prevailing order of thought is a force which brings its like in physical things. If you live in a two dollar per week hall bedroom, and your thought every night and morning is, " Well, I suppose I must always live in this barren den," you are by such despondent state of mind creating in the invisible but most powerful element of thought, a power which will keep you in that room, and in a cheap, inferior corresponding order of life. If you say in your thought, and keep saying it, and keep so far as you can your mind in the state to say this: " I accept this room only as my temporary abode. I will have a better one, and after that a better one still, and everything else better," you are then, through the mysterious agency of your own thought power, bringing the better to you. You have then set a magnet as real, though invisible, as the loadstone at work drawing the better to you, and you will find, as this state of mind is persisted in, that you will gradually drift away from cheap and relatively unsuccessful people into a more aspiring, broader, and successful order of mind.

June 9th

Joseph Murphy

You must realize by now that your conscious mind is the "watchman at the gate," and its chief function is to protect your subconscious mind from false impressions. You are now aware of one of the basic laws of mind: Your subconscious mind is amenable to suggestion. As you know, your subconscious mind does not make comparisons, or contrasts, neither does it reason and think things out for itself. This latter function belongs to your conscious mind. It simply reacts to the impressions given to it by your conscious mind. It does not show a preference for one course of action over another.

June 10th

Ernest Holmes

One of the things which greatly hinders us from demonstrating a greater degree of prosperity we may call race thought or race consciousness. This is the result of all that the race has thought or believed. We are immersed in it, and those who are receptive to it are controlled by it. All thought seeks expression along the lines of least resistance. When we become negative or fearful we attract that kind of thought and condition. We must be sure of ourselves; we must be positive; we must not be aggressive, but absolutely sure and poised within. Negative people are always picking up negative conditions; they get into trouble easily: Persons who are positive draw positive things; they are always successful. Few people realize that the law of thought is the great reality; that thoughts produce things. When we come to understand this power of thought, we will carefully watch our thinking to see that no thought enters that we should not want made into a thing.

June 11th

Helen Wilmans

It is entirely proper to treat sickness and death as beliefs, because a man is a mental creature, and all his conditions are beliefs; but beliefs are real conditions. A belief that is based on the great foundation theory of this or past ages, that evil is a self-existent force, must necessarily be a negative belief because it rests on a mistake. It has not the solid basis of absolute truth on which to rest, and from which it is fed constantly. It is like the house built on sand, which, when the rains descend and the floods come, is washed away, and the world sees it no more. But the beliefs which rest upon that incontrovertible and universal truth — all is good, or Life — are positive; they cannot be shaken; they are fed every instant by an influx of new truth, and they become stronger and stronger, building him who entertains them into splendid health and strength and beauty and courage; carrying him every moment farther away from the possibilities of ever again dropping into the negative condition where sickness and death can master him.

June 12th

Uriel Buchanan

Love others as you would have them love you, and fear not to let them feel and see the warmth and sunlight you hold for them. Remember that thousands are crushed and discouraged because of the world's indifference and coldness, needing but a word, spoken by a friend in tones of sympathy, to fire them with renewed strength to push forward and win. Keep the body and mind in touch with the spirit of harmony. The blue of the sky, the colors of the rainbow, and the blending of shades where the air and sunshine kiss waving grass and graceful foliage are the visible expressions of the law of harmony as manifested through nature. Likewise the glow of the cheek, the brightness of the eye, the quick step and graceful bearing reveal the divine self expressing its harmonies through the most wonderful instrument of a supreme creation. With the consciousness of power, the love for high attainment and the unwavering resolve, there must also be faith in the harmony and goodness of the laws and forces you invoke to your aid. If you remain true to the highest monitions, and are not led astray by the counter influences which constantly appear, if your love for the attainment of the highest and best is greater than your attraction toward all that is unworthy, you will bring to your aid the host of invisible powers which work on the human plane for the upliftment of man. In countless ways you will have unmistakable evidence of help from unseen sources, which will strengthen your faith in the divine leadings and give courage to reach up and attain. Let your watchword be onward, and turn not back; but with your eyes fixed on the final goal, with uplifted, eager hands, continue to tread the path which leads towards the heights; and know that the time will come when that mysterious force within you, which now causes the heart to beat with infinite longings, will not be silenced until you have received response to every yearning and realized the fulfillment of every hope.

June 13th

Christian Larson

There are a number of ways through which our selected thoughts, images, pictures and impressions may be placed in the mind — and placed deeply. The first is definite purpose. Anything that we purpose to do, learn or accomplish will impress itself upon the mind — provided we purpose with the whole heart, and for some time. And, according to the law, that is what the creative power of the mind will work for. It is the height of wisdom therefore, to purpose, with the whole heart, to achieve and realize the very best that life has to offer. The creative power within will, thereby, produce, in us and for us, more and more of the best as time goes on. We will accomplish more and become more; and a better future will unfold. The second way or method is found in positive expectation. What we continue to expect, deeply and positively, will impress itself in the mind, and receive the full attention of creative power. That is why we usually get what we expect; and why we should never expect anything but the best — both for ourselves and for others. The rule is this: what we continue to expect, the creative power of the mind will work for; and what that power works for, will be realized in time — possibly, in a short time. That power is great enough to work out anything, or cause anything to come true. Appreciating this aspect of the law, we all should place before the mind, and in the mind, a number of great expectations; and it would be an excellent plan to write out a program of great expectations — the best and the most wonderful that we could possibly vision, and for all phases of life — present and future. We should concentrate on this program daily — with tremendous interest and enthusiasm — deeply intent on realizing them all. These expectations would be worked for, behind the scenes in the mind, and one after the other would come true.

June 14th

Ernest Holmes

We can draw from the Infinite only as much as we first think into it. It is at this point that so many fail, thinking that all they need to do is to affirm what they want and it will follow. While it is true that affirmations have real power, it is also true that they have only that which we speak into them. As we cannot speak a word that we do not know, so we cannot make an affirmation that we do not understand. We really affirm only that which we know to be true; we know that to be true which we have experienced within ourselves. Although we may have heard or read that this or that thing is true, it is only when there is something within our own souls that corresponds or recognizes its truth, that it is true to us. This ought never to be lost sight of: we can effectively affirm only that which we know, and we know only that which we are. It is herein that we see the necessity of providing within a greater concept of life; a bigger idea of ourselves and a more expanded concept of the Universe in which we live, move and have our being. This is a matter of inner growth together with the enlarging of all lines of thought and activity.

June 15th

Venice J. Bloodworth

The Universal Mind is Omnipotent and Omnipresent: It surrounds you like the sunshine and air. Your Subconscious Mind is part of the Universal Mind and through your Subconscious self you have access to the mighty wisdom and power of the Universal Mind. When you realize this fact there is no limit to your achievement. For the mind does its building solely by the power of thought. Its creations take form in exact accord with your mental image, and desire builds the mental image for you. This is the secret of the power of prayer. God is not a being to be flattered or bought by promises into granting your desires. If that were true every man would receive his wish for there is no one living who has not prayed for something. When you pray earnestly you form a mental image of what you want, and if your faith is strong enough you hold your desire in your thoughts; then the Universal Mind works with you and for you, thus bringing your desire into manifestation. If you are lacking in material wealth or lacking in health, it is because you do not believe or you do not understand your own power. It is not a question of God giving you your heart's desire — EVERYTHING IS OMNIPRESENT FOR EVERYBODY — You have only to realize your own power and use it.

June 16th

James Allen

One cannot alter external things to suit his passing whims and wishes, but he can set aside his whims and wishes; he can so alter his attitude of mind towards externals that they will assume a different aspect. He cannot mould the actions of others towards him, but he can rightly fashion his actions towards them. He cannot break down the wall of circumstance by which he is surrounded, but he can wisely adapt himself to it, or find the way out into enlarged circumstances by extending his mental horizon. Things follow thoughts. Alter your thoughts, and things will receive a new adjustment. To reflect truly the mirror must be true. A warped glass gives back an exaggerated image. A disturbed mind gives a distorted reflection of the world. Subdue the mind, organize and tranquillize it, and a more beautiful image of the universe, a more prefect perception of the world-order will be the result.

June 17th

Robert Collier

When a man realizes that his mind is part of Universal Mind, when he realizes that he has only to take any right aspiration to this Universal Mind to see it realized, he loses all sense of worry and fear. He learns to dominate instead of to cringe. He rises to meet every situation, secure in the knowledge that everything necessary to the solution of any problem is in Mind, and that he has but to take his problem to Universal Mind to have it correctly answered. For if you take a drop of water from the ocean, you know that it has the same properties as all the rest of the water in the ocean, the same percentage of sodium chloride. The only difference between it and the ocean is in volume. If you take a spark of electricity, you know that it has the same properties as the thunderbolt, the same power that moves trains or runs giant machines in factories. Again the only difference is in volume. It is the same with your mind and Universal Mind. The only difference between them is in volume. Your mind has the same properties as the Universal Mind, the same creative genius, the same power over all the earth, the same access to all knowledge. Know this, believe it, use it, and "yours is the earth and the fullness thereof." In the exact proportion that you believe yourself to be part of Universal Mind, sharing in Its all-power, in that proportion can you demonstrate the mastery over your own body and over the world about you.

June 18th

Ernest Holmes

Nothing can happen to us that is not first an accepted belief in our own consciousness. We may not always be aware of what is going on within, but practice will enable us to control our thought more and more so that we shall be able to think what we want to think, regardless of what may seem to be the case. Each person has within himself the capacity of knowing and making use of the law but it must be consciously developed. This is done by practice, and by willingness to learn and to utilize whatever we know so far as we have gone. The individual who has the most power is the one who has the greatest realization of the Divine Presence, and to whom this means the most as an active principle of his life. We all need more backbone and less wishbone. There is something which waits only our recognition to spring into being, bringing with it all the power in the universe.

June 19th

Christian Larson

Whatever a man desires to do, if he thinks that he can, he will develop the necessary power, and when the necessary power and ability are gained, the tangible results inevitably follow. The secret is persistence. After you have decided what you want to do, begin to think that you can, and continue without ceasing to think that you can. Pay no attention to temporary failures; know that you can, and continue to think that you can. To continue in the consciousness of the law that underlies this idea will bring greater results and more rapid results, because in that case you will consciously direct the developing process, and you will know that to think you can is to develop the power that can. To keep constantly before mind the idea that "he can who thinks he can," will steadily increase the qualities of faith, self-confidence, perseverance and persistence; and whoever develops these qualities to a greater and greater degree will move forward without fail. Therefore, to live in the conviction that "he can who thinks he can," will not only increase ability along the desired lines, but will also produce the power to push that ability into a living, tangible action. In addition to thinking that you can do, try to do; put into practice at once what power and ability you possess, and by continuing to think that you can do more, you will develop the power to do more. To keep before mind the idea that "he can who thinks he can" will also hold attention upon the high ideals we have in view, and this is extremely important.

June 20th

Joseph Murphy

Peace of mind and a healthy body are inevitable when you begin to think and feel in the right way. Whatever you claim mentally and feel as true, your subconscious mind will accept and bring forth into your experience. The only thing necessary for you to do is to get your subconscious mind to accept your idea, and the law of your own subconscious mind will bring forth the health, peace, or the position you desire. You give the command or decree, and your subconscious will faithfully reproduce the idea impressed upon it. The law of your mind is this: You will get a reaction or response from your subconscious mind according to the nature of the thought or idea you hold in your conscious mind.

June 21st

Joseph Murphy

"And he saith unto them Draw out now, and bear unto the governor of the feast." Whatever is impregnated in our subconscious mind is always objectified on the screen of space; consequently, when we enter a state of conviction that our prayer is answered, we have given the command, "Bear unto the governor of the feast." You are always governing your mental feast. During the day thousands of thoughts, suggestions, opinions, sights, and sounds reach your eyes and ears. You can reject them as unfit for mental consumption or entertain them, as you choose. Your conscious, reasoning, intellectual mind is the governor of the feast. When you consciously choose to entertain, meditate, feast upon, and imagine your heart's desire as true, it becomes a living embodiment and a part of your mentality, so that your deeper self gives birth or expression to it. In other words, what is impressed subjectively is expressed objectively. Your senses or conscious mind see the objectification of your good. When the conscious mind becomes aware of "water made into wine," it becomes aware of the answered prayer. Water might be called, also, the invisible, formless, spiritual power, unconditioned consciousness. Wine is conditioned consciousness, or the mind giving birth to its beliefs and convictions.

June 22nd

Ernest Holmes

To the student who has realized that all is mind and that everything is governed by law, there comes another thought: it is that he can create, or have created for him, from his own thinking. He can create such a strong mental atmosphere of success that its power of attraction will be irresistible. He can send his thought throughout the world and have it bring back to him whatever he wants. He can so fill his place of business with the power of success that it will draw from far and near. Thought will always bring back to us what we send out. First we must clear our thought of all unbelief. This book (Creative Mind and Success) is written for those who believe; and to those who do believe it will come true in their lives. Without mental clearness on the part of the thinker there can be no real creative work done. As water will reach only its own level, so mind will return to us only what we first believe. We are always getting what we believe but not always what we want. Our thought has the power to reach, in the outer form of conditions, an exact correspondence to our inner convictions.

June 23rd

Joseph Murphy

What, in your opinion, is the master secret of the ages? The secret of atomic energy? Thermonuclear energy? The neutron bomb? Interplanetary travel? No — not any of these. Then, what is this master secret? Where can one find it, and how can it be contacted and brought into action? The answer is extraordinarily simple. This secret is the marvelous, miracle-working power found in your own subconscious mind, the last place that most people would seek it.

June 24th

Uriel Buchanan

The great starting point to freedom and power is the conservation of force. Force is omnipresent. The most important problem is not how to get force, but how to conserve, arouse and wisely direct the force already at command. The physical organism is like an engine, and the mind is the engineer. If the boiler is full of holes, the force will be dissipated, and the machine cannot do effective work. You must stop the leakage, the useless waste by dissipation, and the worry and discontent arising from a distorted imagination. You must cultivate more constructive thought and put vital force into all your actions. You must learn to concentrate the mind to the consideration of a single thing, at any given time, to the exclusion of all else. And everything you do should be a stepping stone to some fruitful end. The mind must become steadfast and unwavering, and your thoughts creative, expressing the highest and best within. Only as you have health and happiness and use the force of body and faculties of mind aright can you rise to the threshold of the perfect way. You are by the attitude of thought you hold always drawing to you corresponding conditions which are beneficial or injurious. There is a mental state which, if permanently held to, will draw to you all that is desirable. If you are always calm and determined and have an unwavering purpose, you will attract to you from the invisible domain the things you silently demand. But if you lack faith and are haunted by fear and uncertainty, you will drive happiness from you and will attract misfortune and failure. Whatever you think you actually make a reality in the realm of mind. If you hold the same thought through days and months and years you give the idea tangible form. If you keep the idea of success in your mind, and dwell on thoughts whose aim is good, you set in motion the attractive force which goes out in the unseen and influences material agencies to serve you. And the longer your mental forces are fixed on the bright and beautiful, on success and happiness, the more power you will have to draw health and prosperity to you. To fix your mind persistently on some definite purpose, to resolve that nothing shall interfere, that you will have the thing desired, maintaining the mood of calm, patient determination, you will grow in possibilities not yet dreamed of.

June 25th

Christian Larson

If it is your belief that there is nothing in your life for which you can justly be glad, stop and count your blessings. You will surprise yourself; and you will then and there resolve never to depreciate yourself again. Henceforth, you will find it easier to be glad; and you will also find that the more things you are glad for, the more things you will have to be glad for. Gladness is a magnet and it draws more and more of everything that can increase gladness. Just be glad always and under every circumstance, and nothing shall be withheld from you that can add to your welfare and happiness. Should you find it easy to be glad when things go right, and difficult to be glad when things go wrong, you are not creating your own sunshine; and it is only the sunshine that we create ourselves, in our own world, that makes things grow in our own world. Be glad because you want to be glad, regardless of events, and you will have found that fountain of joy within that is ever ready to overflow. Be glad at all times because it is best to be glad at all times; and be glad in the presence of everything because gladness makes it better for everything. Just be glad, and the world will be kind to you. The sunbeam has no occasion for regrets. It is always welcome; it is always loved. Just be glad, and you will have friends without number; and it is he who has many friends, friends that are good and true, who finds everything that is rich and beautiful in human existence. Just be glad, and you will be sought for, far and wide. The world is not looking for gloom and depression; it is looking for sunshine and joy.

June 26th

Ernest Holmes

All is mind, and we must provide a receptive avenue for it as it passes out through us into the outer expression of our affairs. If we allow the world's opinion to control our thinking, then that will be our demonstration. If, on the other hand, we rise superior to the world, we shall do a new thing. Remember that all people are making demonstrations, only most of them are making the ones they do not desire, but the only ones they can make with their present powers of perception.

June 27th

Prentice Mulford

When people come together and in any way talk out their ill-will towards others they are drawing to themselves with tenfold power an injurious thought current. Because the more minds united on any purpose the more power do they attract to effect that purpose. The thought current so attracted by those chronic complainers, grumblers and scandal mongers, will injure their bodies. Because whatever thought is most held in mind is most materialized in the body. If we are always thinking and talking of people's imperfections we are drawing to us ever of that thought current, and thereby incorporating into ourselves those very imperfections.

June 28th

Venice J. Bloodworth

The subconscious mind within each of us (Holy Spirit or God) is a vast magnet, with the power to draw from Universal Mind (God) all that we want. Don't be afraid to ask for a car, a new house, or a diamond ring. If those are the things you want — they are already yours for the asking. There is NO LIMIT to what God can give you — the only limitation is in yourself — yourself — YOUR ABILITY TO RECEIVE. When confronted with any particular desire, I say: "I AM an irresistible magnet with the power to draw unto myself everything I desire. My Father's storehouse has all abundance and there is unlimited supply (or money) available to me right now. I claim (my desire) as mine already, and that I shall very soon tangibly realize its possession. If there is anything you wish me to do, Father, give me a definite lead." Having spoken the word, rest content. The Spirit is doing the work. Do not try to buy a car, for instance, by wondering if father, mother, or husband can be prevailed upon to give you so and so. You have no right to try and wrest from another what is rightfully theirs. If that is God's means of supplying you in that particular instance, he will open the way without any effort from you. You have just as great a share in His storehouse as father, mother or husband, and His ideas for supplying you with your share of His riches are legion. Trust Him — it pays. "Prove me now herewith, saith the Lord of Hosts, if I will not open you the windows of heaven and pour you out a blessing that there shall not be room to receive." Do not make hard work of attaining this spiritual heritage of ours. Our Father has given us the Kingdom, only asking in return that we become as little children and "Fear not, only believe."

June 29th

Joseph Murphy

The body of man portrays the workings of his inner mind. Our real powers are resident in the subconscious mind. No one knows all of the workings of the subconscious mind; for it is infinite in its scope. We learn what we can about how it works; then we use it accordingly. People say there is an intelligence which will take care of the body if we let it alone. This is true, but the difficulty is that the conscious mind always interferes with its five-sense evidence based on outer appearances, leading to the sway of false beliefs, fears, and mere opinion. When fear, false beliefs, and negative patterns are made to register in the subconscious mind through psychological, emotional conditioning, there is no other course open to the subconscious mind except to act on the blueprint specification offered to it. The subjective self within you works continuously for the general good, reflecting an innate principle of harmony behind all things. Study the works of Edison, Carver, Einstein, and many others who without too much outer education knew how to tap the subconscious mind for its manifold treasures. Have a reason for the faith in you. You cannot get very far if you do not believe in what you do not see. I do not see love, but I feel it; I do not see beauty, I see it manifested. Subjective faith is often greater in a puny body of a garret-loving poet than in the stronger frame of a prize fighter. Our greatest failing is a lack of confidence in the powers of the subconscious mind. Get acquainted with your inner powers.

June 30th

Ernest Holmes

The soul that knows its own Divinity is the great soul; before it all else must bend; to it all else must gravitate. Enlarge your thought processes. Away with the little personal thoughts of things, and dare to think in universal terms about all things. The universe is running over with good, it is for you, but you must believe and then take it. Do you dare to believe that your own word is invincible? When you speak it how do you feel? Is it limitless, is it all power, is all power given to you in heaven and on earth. are you one with the only power that there is? Until you can say yes to all these questions and not simply believe them but know them, you cannot hope to attain. It is useless in making a demonstration to beg for things; as well beg that water should be wet or that fire should be hot. Things are, we must take them. Your word has only the power that you put into it, no more and no less. We are all held accountable for every word that we speak because all is the action and the reaction of mind. Man is his own heaven and his own hell.

July

July 1st

Christian Larson

Thoughts inspired by environment are inferior or superior, according to what the environment may be; but an original thought is always superior, because it is inspired by man himself while the superior elements of his being are predominant. When every thought that mind creates is an original thought, man will constantly grow in greatness, superiority and worth; and when all these original thoughts are created with the same purpose in view, man will become exactly what is indicated by that purpose. Therefore, since man can base thinking upon any purpose that he may desire, he can, through original thinking, become whatever he may choose to become. Fate is the result of man's being and doing; a direct effect of the life and the works of the individual; a natural creation of man; and the creation is always the image and likeness of the creator. Therefore, when man, through original thinking, acquires the power to become what he chooses to become, his fate will of itself change as man changes; and through this law he can create for himself any fate desired. That man will consciously and naturally create his own fate when he gains the power to recreate himself as he desires to be, is evident for various reasons. And the power to recreate himself is simply the power of original thought. Because man becomes like the thoughts he thinks, and original thoughts are created in the likeness of man's ideal impressions of his superior self.

July 2nd

Genevieve Behrend

Troward says the "Mental faculties always work under something which stimulates them, and this stimulus may come either from without, through the external senses, or from within, by the consciousness of something not perceptible on the physical plane. The recognition of this interior source of stimulus enables you to bring into your consciousness any state you desire." Once a thing seems normal to you, it is as surely yours, through the Law of growth and attraction, as it is yours to know addition after you have learned the use of figures. This method of repeating the word makes the word in all of its limitless meaning yours, because words are the embodiment of thoughts, and thought is creative; neither good nor bad, simply creative. This is the reason why Faith builds up and Fear destroys. "Only believe, and all things are possible unto you." It is Faith that gives you dominion over every adverse circumstance or condition. It is your word of Faith that sets you free; not faith in any specific thing or act, but simple Faith in your best self in all ways. It is this ever-present Creative Power within the heart of the word that makes your health, your peace of mind, and your financial condition a reproduction of your most habitual thought. Try to believe and understand this, and you will find yourself Master of every adverse circumstance or condition, for you will become a Prince of Power.

July 3rd

James Allen

The body is the image of the mind, and in it are traced the visible features of hidden thoughts. The outer obeys the inner, and the enlightened scientist of the future may be able to trace every bodily disorder to its ethical cause in the mentality. Mental harmony, or moral wholeness, makes for bodily health. I say makes for it, for it will not produce it magically, as it were — as though one should swallow a bottle of medicine and then be whole and free — but if the mentality is becoming more poised and restful, if the moral stature is increasing, then a sure foundation of bodily wholeness is being laid, the forces are being conserved and are receiving a better direction and adjustment; and even if perfect health is not gained, the bodily derangement, whatever it be, will have lost its power to undermine the strengthened and uplifted mind.

July 4th

Ernest Holmes

There should be absolutely no sense of responsibility beyond speaking the word in positive faith, knowing. All struggle belongs to the Old Order; in the New peace takes the place of confusion, faith answers the cry of doubt and fear, and the Word is supreme. We must know that our word is law, and cannot be set aside by the false thought of the world. Every time that we state a truth, we must know that that truth destroys all that is unlike itself and frees the thought of the one whom we wish to help and to heal. This word must become the new Law which frees. People are sick because they think sickness and will be healed only when they turn from this kind of thought and begin to think in terms of health.

July 5th

Joseph Murphy

You have a mind, and you should learn how to use it. There are two levels of your mind — the conscious or rational level, and the subconscious or irrational level. You think with your conscious mind, and whatever you habitually think sinks down into your subconscious mind, which creates according to the nature of your thoughts. Your subconscious mind is the seat of your emotions and is the creative mind. If you think good, good will follow; if you think evil, evil will follow. This is the way your mind works. The main point to remember is once the subconscious mind accepts an idea, it begins to execute it. It is an interesting and subtle truth that the law of the subconscious mind works for good and bad ideas alike. This law, when applied in a negative way, is the cause of failure, frustration, and unhappiness. However, when your habitual thinking is harmonious and constructive, you experience perfect health, success, and prosperity.

July 6th

Uriel Buchanan

We have learned that there is no avenging Deity, no stern judge sitting on his throne in the supreme court of heaven, whose chief pleasure consists in punishing humanity for every violation of law, we know that the universe is governed by the Infinite Spirit of Love, which constantly inspires to greater goodness, purity and unselfishness, lifting us up to a happier and finer state of being. Every noble impulse awakens a multitude of helpful thoughts which rush to us to give strength and encouragement, while every evil thought or act is instantly rebuked by the monitor within, from whose judgment there is no escaping. To obtain more of the spirit of love, to acquire power from the Infinite Source, to grow in knowledge and wisdom and overcome the defects of our nature, we must have a mind that ever aspires to the highest and best. As a part of the Infinite Mind, we should reach up and demand what we most need. We will have power to obtain results in proportion to the force and earnestness of our thought and desire. Persistent earnest desire is a magnetic power which, when encouraged by faith and strengthened by effort, will invariably draw to you the thing wished for. Every obstacle that is conquered, every new victory gained, will give you more faith in your power, and you will have greater ability to win.

July 7th

Christian Larson

To master fate it is necessary to approach all the elements of fate in the proper mental attitudes; because since everything in the external world responds to the active forces in one's mental world, these forces should so act as to call forth only the response desired. The idea of mastery will arouse in the average mind a tendency to control objective things with the will; but we must remember that fate is not controlled; fate is created. When we can create any fate that we may desire, we have mastered fate; but not until then. The mastery of fate does not call for the controlling actions of the will, but for the constructive actions of the creative energies; and since the domineering use of the will scatters creative energy, such an attitude of mind must never be permitted. All desire to control or influence persons or things must be eliminated completely, because such a course will only defeat our purpose. We do not master fate by compelling things to come our way; or by persuading persons to promote our objects in view. Things will come of themselves when we demonstrate our ability to use things; and persons will cooperate with us in every way possible when we prove the superiority of both ourselves and our work. The weakest mind of all is the domineering mind, and since such a mind has but little creative energy, the man who domineers cannot fulfill, legitimately, a single desire. And what he does control through force, will later on react to his own downfall.

July 8th

Ernest Holmes

Did you ever see the law that causes a plant to grow? Of course you did not, and yet you believe in this hidden law of growth. Why do you believe? Simply because every year, out of the seed time comes a harvest. Shall we not have as great faith in the higher laws of being? To those souls who have dared to believe has come as definite an answer as came to those who believed in receiving a harvest from the planted seed. This law is, and if we would see results we must use it; that is, we must provide the mental receptivity that will prepare us to accept the gift when the Spirit makes it. This receiving is a mental process, a process in which we lose all sense of limitation.

July 9th

Robert Collier

I must give to every human being I come in contact with, from my wife to the bootblack who shines my shoes; from my brother to my sworn foe. Sometimes people will tell you to smile; but the smile I give has got to be a real smile that lives up to its advertising. If I go around grinning like a Cheshire cat, the Cheshire-cat grin will be what I get back — multiplied! If I give the real thing, I'll get back the real thing — multiplied! If anybody objects that this is a selfish view to take, I answer him that any law of salvation from anything by anybody that has ever been offered for any purpose, is a selfish view to take. The only unselfishness that has ever been truly taught is that of giving a lesser thing in hope of receiving a greater. "Now, why am I so sure of this law? How can you be sure? I have watched it work; it works everywhere. You have only to try it, and keep on trying it and it will prove true for you. It is not true because I say so, nor because anybody else says so; it is just true. Theosophists call it the law of Karma; humanitarians call it the law of Service; business men call it the law of common sense; Jesus Christ called it the law of Love. It rules whether I know it or not, whether I believe it or not, whether I defy it or not. I can't break it! Jesus of Nazareth, without reference to any religious idea you may have about Him, without consideration as to whether He was or was not divine, was the greatest business Man that ever lived, and he said: 'Give and ye shall receive — good measure, pressed down, shaken together, running over!' And this happens to be so — not because He said it — but because it is the Truth.

July 10th

Venice J. Bloodworth

IN ALL ages people have believed in a Magic Word, because, wise men and prophets have spoken of the "Power of the Word." The Fable of Ali Baba and the Forty Thieves, with the magic word "Sesame," is based on this belief. Naturally the majority of us today know that no one word could be vested with any unusual power, but what the majority do not know is that EVERY WORD YOU SPEAK IS A WORD OF POWER IN EXACT ACCORD WITH YOUR OWN CONSCIOUS POWER. Develop your knowledge of your own power and WATCH YOUR AFFIRMATIONS COME TRUE, not only for yourself but for others whom you wish to help. "In the beginning was the word," or the beginning of everything is thought, and as every thought must be clothed in words the beginning of everything is the word. SO YOUR WORD IS THE WORD OF

POWER, and whether you speak from the house tops or speak in the recesses of your own soul — your body and environment will certainly and surely reflect what you ARE. In every line of this work I have told you the same truth. You can be healthy, happy, and successful by your own efforts and no real or lasting good can come to you except as it reflects your own state of mind.

July 11th

Joseph Murphy

William James, the father of American psychology, said that the power to move the world is in your subconscious mind. Your subconscious mind is one with infinite intelligence and boundless wisdom. It is fed by hidden springs, and is called the law of life. Whatever you impress upon your subconscious mind, the latter will move heaven and earth to bring it to pass. You must, therefore, impress it with right ideas and constructive thoughts. The reason there is so much chaos and misery in the world is because people do not understand the interaction of their conscious and subconscious minds. When these two principles work in accord, in concord, in peace, and synchronously together, you will have heath, happiness, peace and joy. There is no sickness or discord when the conscious and subconscious work together harmoniously and peacefully.

July 12th

Ernest Holmes

The store house of nature is filled with infinite good awaiting the touch of our awakened thought to spring forth into manifestation in our life; but the awakening must be on our part and not on the side of life. We stand at the gateway of limitless opportunity in the eternal and changeless NOW. Now is the day in which to begin the new life that is to lift us up to the greater expression of all that is wonderful. The word that we speak is the Law of our life and nothing hinders but ourselves. We have through ignorance of our real nature misused the power of our word, and behold what it has brought upon us, "the very thing that we feared." But now it shall produce a new thing, a new heaven and a new earth.

July 13th

Christian Larson

Man is ever in search of strength. It is the strong man that wins. It is the man with power that scales the heights. To be strong is to be great; and it is the privilege of greatness to satisfy every desire, every aspiration, every need. But strength is not for the few alone; it is for all, and the way to strength is simple. Proceed this very moment to the mountain tops of the strength you now possess, and whatever may happen do not come down. Do not weaken under adversity. Resolve to remain as strong, as determined and as highly enthused during the darkest night of adversity as you are during the sunniest day of prosperity. Do not feel disappointed when things seem disappointing. Keep the eye single upon the same brilliant future regardless of circumstances, conditions or events. Do not lose heart when things go wrong. Continue undisturbed in your original resolve to make all things go right. To be overcome by adversity and threatening failure is to lose strength; to always remain in the same lofty, determined mood is to constantly grow in strength. The man who never weakens when things are against him will grow stronger and stronger until all things will delight to be for him. He will finally have all the strength he may desire or need. Be always strong and you will always be stronger.

July 14th

Prentice Mulford

If but two people were to meet at regular intervals and talk of health, strength and vigor of body and mind, at the same time opening their minds to receive of the Supreme the best idea as to the ways and means for securing these blessings, they would attract to them a thought current of such idea. If these two people or more kept up these conversations on these subjects at a regular time and place, and found pleasure in such communings, and they were not forced or stilted; if they could carry them on without controversy, and enter into them without preconceived idea, and not allow any shade of tattle or tale-bearing, or censure of others to drift into their talk, they would be astonished at the year's end at the beneficial results to mind and body. Because in so doing and coming together with a silent demand of the Supreme to get the best idea, they would attract to them a current of Life-giving force. Let two so commence rather than more. For even two persons in the proper agreement and accord to bring the desired results are not easy to find. The desire for such meetings must be spontaneous, and any other motive will bar out the highest thought current for good.

July 15th

Orison Swett Marden

The man who smiles and sees the best in everything and everybody is the man who draws the best out of others. He attracts others and wins out in life, while the gloomy, sour face repels everyone. "No smiles, no business," is the motto of a successful business house. At first this struck me as rather a peculiar motto, but on second thought, I realized how apt it is. Do we not all know that sour, gloomy faces drive away business, and that pleasant, sunny faces attract it? Cheerfulness will attract more customers, sell more goods, do more business with less wear and tear than any other quality. Nobody but himself may be helped by the money millionaire, but everybody is enriched who knows or comes in contact with the millionaire of good cheer, and the more he gives of his wealth the more it multiplies. Andrew Carnegie owed his popularity and much of his success and happiness to his cheerful disposition. In his later years he said: "My young partners do the work and I do the laughing, and I commend to you the thought that there is very little success where there is little laughter." Whoever strikes the keynote of joy and happiness is a dispenser of the balm of Gilead, of a healing force. A man without cheerfulness is a sick man. The sadness of his spirit lays a withering blight on all the beauty of his life. He becomes prematurely old. His strength decays. "A broken spirit drieth up the bones."

July 16th

Ernest Holmes

We are not dealing with a negative as well as a positive Power — not two powers but one; a power that sees neither good nor evil, as we see it. It knows only that it is all, and since it is all, it creates whatever is given it. From our limited standpoint we often think of good, and evil; not realizing that, as yet, we do not know the one from the other. What we call good today, we may call evil tomorrow, and what we think to be evil today, we may tomorrow proclaim as the greatest good we have known. Not so with the great Universal Power of Mind; It sees only Itself, and Its infinite ability to create. To the thinking person this will mean much; he will see that he is no longer living in a limited universe, a world of powers, but that he is immersed in an Infinite Creative Medium which, because of Its Nature, has to create for him whatever he believes. Jesus understood this, and in a few simple words, laid down the law of life: "It is done unto all people as they believe." This is a great thing to keep in mind. It is done unto us; we do not have to do it, for it is done unto us of a power that knows itself to be all there is. Could we even believe that some material mountain would be moved, the power is there to do it. Without this belief there is no real impulse for the Creative Mind, and we do not get an affirmative answer. We must realize more clearly that this Great Power has to operate through us.

July 17th

James Allen

A man is only powerless to overcome the wrong and unhappy elements in himself so long as he regards himself as powerless. If to the bad habit is added the thought "I cannot" the bad habit will remain. Nothing can be overcome till the thought of powerlessness is uprooted and abolished from the mind. The great stumbling-block is not the habit itself, it is the belief in the impossibility of overcoming it. How can a man overcome a bad habit so long as he is convinced that it is impossible? How can a man be prevented from overcoming it when he knows that he can, and is determined to do it? The dominant thought by which man has enslaved himself is the thought "I cannot overcome my sins." Bring this thought out into the light, in all its nakedness, and it is seen to be a belief in the power of evil, with its other pole, disbelief in the power of good. For a man to say, or believe, that he cannot rise above wrong-thinking and wrong-doing, is to submit to evil, is to abandon and renounce good.

July 18th

Joseph Murphy

Your subconscious mind is never short of ideas; there are within it an infinite number of ideas ready to flow into your conscious mind, and appear as cash in your pocket book in countless ways. This process will continue to go on in your mind regardless of whether the market goes up or down, or whether the pound sterling or dollar drops in value. Your wealth is never truly dependent on bonds, stocks, or money in a bank; these are really all symbols necessary and useful, of course. The point I wish to emphasize is that if you convince your subconscious mind that wealth is yours, and that plenty of money is always circulating in your life, you will always have it regardless of the form it takes.

July 19th

Venice J. Bloodworth

If you can truly believe that you have received something, your subconscious mind will surely see that you get it. Everyone who has reaped success has started out to accomplish just one thing. Find out what you want, imagine things as you want them, build new ideas of life, stop believing that some people are lucky and some must be poor, change your ideas and find that life is a beautiful adventure, that each day brings new opportunities to those who will lift their eyes above the everyday grind. Life means something more than animal existence. Get out of the rut, for rut is only another name for "grave." Did not the Master say, "Let the dead bury the dead, come thou and follow me." If you believe in poverty, misery and distress, you are as good as dead already.

July 20th

Ernest Holmes

The great law of life is thinking and becoming; and when we think from the lofty heights of the Spirit we will become great, and not until then. Do not try to convince any one of the truth; that will bring confusion. Truth is, just as much as God is; and the whole world is coming gradually into the realization of it. Keep the truth within your own soul, lift your own self above the confusion of life, and then people will believe. So all our thought is to be created in the realization of the One becoming the many, without struggle, without fear; stripped of all that denies the truth.

July 21st

Christian Larson

The creative power of the mind will work for that which we believe in, and according to the same law. We should never believe, therefore, in trouble, failure, calamity, disaster, nor the coming of the worst. We do not want the great power to work for those things, and thus help to bring them to pass. We should believe in the very best, and the greatest, in every mode and manner — and for everybody. We should believe in better conditions, greater achievements and a more wonderful future; and in these possibilities we should believe tremendously. There is a saying to this effect: "When you believe it absolutely — then it happens." And now we know why such a startling statement can be true. What we believe in absolutely, is placed deeply and permanently in the mind. What we place deeply and permanently in the mind, the creative power within will work for continuously, and with full capacity. The results are inevitable; for that power is great enough to do anything. This creative power within always works for that which we are determined to have. That is why we usually get, sooner or later, what we continue to determine that we shall have. Our determinations, however, must be deep, and without ceasing. Creative power will work only for those things that are placed deeply in the mind. This explains why so many fail to get results. They live and think on the surface only. They do not place their thoughts and impressions deeply in the mind.

July 22nd

Uriel Buchanan

The universal will, acting through man as directed by thought and desire, enables him to control the forces of nature and to use the ether of space as a medium for conveying his message and command to the most distant parts of the world. By the power of his will man should dispel fear and uncertainty and assume the dignity of his rightful place. The degree of man's success is determined by the nature and intensity of desire and the strength of his will. The will concentrates into a tiny cell the immensities of the universe. Fundamentally it is identical with universal life, acting in us either consciously or unconsciously, natural or unnatural, as determined by choice and desire. Concentration of will power and harmonic mental action, impelled by persistent desire, will remove all barriers and make a straight pathway to the highest goal. The will should be disciplined to work incessantly for the right and good. You should refuse to recognize all that is useless, selfish or sordid. You should direct your forces unerringly to study and self development. You should be filled with a determination to do that which you recognize as necessary to the highest attainment. The will should be thoroughly understood and subjected to the severest scrutiny. The earnest desire to live in harmony with the higher laws will gradually emancipate the mind and give invincible courage.

July 23rd

Robert Collier

What do you lack? What thing do you want most? Realize that before it or any other thing can be, it must first be imaged in Mind. Realize, too, that when you can close your eyes and actually SEE that thing, you have brought it into being — you have drawn upon that invisible substance all about you — you have created something. Hold it in your thought, focus your mind upon it, "BELIEVE THAT YOU HAVE IT" — and you can safely leave its material manifestation to the Genie-of-your-Mind. God is but another name for the invisible, everywhere-present, Source-of-things. Out of the air the seed gathers the essences which are necessary to its bountiful growth; out of the invisible ether our minds gather the rich ideas that stimulate us to undertake and to carry out enterprises that bring prosperity to us. Let us see with the eye of the mind a bountiful harvest; then our minds will be quickened with ideas of abundance, and plenty will appear, not only in our world, but everywhere. "As the rain cometh down and the snow from heaven, and returneth not thither, but watereth the earth, and maketh it bring forth and bud, and giveth seed to the sower and bread to the eater; so shall my word be that goeth forth out of my mouth: it shall not return unto me void, but it shall accomplish that which I please, and it shall prosper in the thing whereto I sent it." — Isaiah.

July 24th

Ernest Holmes

To one who knows the truth, both praise and blame sound alike, but from the human standpoint at least a person cannot help being amused at the way in which the world judges true spirituality. My idea of true spirituality is that a man should live a perfectly normal life, entering into and enjoying all in life that is clean and good. He should place himself absolutely under the divine guidance. Other than this he will seem just like other people, neither better nor worse. Get over all kinds of unnatural thought and remember that all is good. Neither criticize nor condemn people or things. You are spiritual in so far as you trust in the Spirit, at all times, in all places, under all conditions. In order to do this you do not have to seclude yourself from the world. To do so is an open confession of your own weakness and lack. There are moments when it is best to be alone with the Power. From these moments we gather strength. To keep that strength to ourselves is pure selfishness. Walk, talk, live with the human race, hand in hand with all people and unified with all events, live and love and learn. Be natural and normal. If you seek to enter some other way it must all be done over again, for no one lives or dies unto himself but unto all people.

July 25th

Charles F. Haanel

There are many who are not ready to enter into the discipline necessary to think correctly, even though it is evident that wrong thinking has brought failure. Thought is the only reality; conditions are but the outward manifestations; as the thought changes, all outward or material conditions must change in order to be in harmony with their creator, which is thought. But the thought must be clear cut, steady, fixed, definite, unchangeable; you cannot take one step forward and two steps backward, neither can you spend twenty or thirty years of your life building up negative conditions as the result of negative thoughts, and then expect to see them all melt away as the result of fifteen or twenty minutes of right thinking. If you enter into the discipline necessary to bring about a radical change in your life, you must do so deliberately, after giving the matter careful thought and full consideration, and then you must allow nothing to interfere with your decision. This discipline, this change of thought, this mental attitude will not only bring you the material things which are necessary for your highest and best welfare, but will bring health and harmonious conditions generally. If you wish harmonious conditions in your life, you must develop an harmonious mental attitude. Your world without will be a reflection of your world within.

July 26th

Joseph Murphy

Knowledge of the interaction of your conscious and subconscious minds will enable you to transform your whole life. In order to change external conditions, you must change the cause. Most men try to change conditions and circumstances by working with conditions and circumstances. To remove discord, confusion, lack, and limitation, you must remove the cause, and the cause is the way you are using your conscious mind. In other words, the way you are thinking and picturing in your mind. You are living in a fathomless sea of infinite riches. Your subconscious is very sensitive to your thoughts. Your thoughts form the mold or matrix through which the infinite intelligence, wisdom, vital forces, and energies of your subconscious flow.

July 27th

Christian Larson

Fate is created by the powers in man; therefore, in order to master fate, man must acquire control over the creative forces in his being. And this is accomplished, not by trying to control these forces, but by changing their courses. Every force in the system moves through the field of consciousness, and by training the will to act upon consciousness so as to open or close the channels of consciousness in any place, the different forces in the system can be directed wherever desired. No force can be driven. We cannot drive the force of electricity; but by providing suitable conductors, electricity will go wherever it is wanted, because we have the power to move the conductors about as we like. The channels of consciousness, more correctly designated the tendencies of mind, are the conductors of the creative forces of the system; therefore, by regulating the tendencies of mind we may cause all, or any desired part of our creative power to accumulate at any time in any place of mind or body. To regulate the tendencies of mind, the will must act upon the finer or inner side of consciousness; and whatever the will wills to have done while acting upon the finer side, the same will be done. To reach this finer side, mind must enter a perpetual refining process, and must establish this process in every part of the system. Create a strong desire to transform, refine and improve everything with which you come in contact, and the finer consciousness will develop steadily. This is the first essential. The second essential is to properly meet the forces that come into your life, because every force that comes, comes to act; and how it is met will determine whether its action upon you will be favorable or not. When you meet a force, you must do something with it, or it will do something with you; you must direct it, or it will pass through your system aimlessly and be lost. Or, if it is an undeveloped force, as most forces are, you will permit the formation of adverse conditions by permitting such a force to pass through your world unguided. It is the nature of all forces to do things; they cannot be idle; therefore, if you do not give them something definite to build, they will build aimlessly, or destroy ruthlessly.

July 28th

Ernest Holmes

Majestic and calm, waiting with eternal and divine patience, the Great Principle of Life is ready to give to us all that it has. And while we listen and wait we will cast from us everything that hinders its complete expression through us, we will let go of all struggle and all strife and be at peace with Life. Perfect peace to the soul as we rest in the realization of our unity with all that there is, was or ever will be. One with the Infinite Mind. All the power of the Spirit is working through our thought as we believe and receive. Now we will ask for and take that thing which we desire; it is done, it is complete, now and forever. Perfect life, perfect healing, perfect harmony, Divine guidance, Infinite strength and joy forever.

July 29th

Henry Thomas Hamblin

People say: "You can't help thinking these thoughts can you?" They take it for granted that one cannot control one's thoughts. They do not realize that it is possible deliberately to change the subject as regards one's thoughts, in the same way that one changes the topic of conversation. We all of us change the subject of conversation when it becomes distasteful to us, but how many of us change the subject of our thoughts in the same deliberate manner, by the exercise of our will? Yet it can be done, almost as easily, if we will only DO IT, instead of thinking and saying that it cannot be done. Not only is it possible to change the subject of our thoughts, but it is also possible to refrain from thinking altogether. Both are accomplishments of the highest possible value and they can be acquired only by practice and self training; but, even the weakest of us can acquire them if we are quietly persistent. We do not need to be clever, or greatly gifted, or out of the ordinary. Indeed, we may be very much under the average in mental gifts, will power and intellectual endowments; yet, if we are quietly persistent, we can learn to overcome our thoughts, in course of time. And when we become master of our thoughts we become master of ourselves, and when we become master of ourselves we become master of life itself; not by opposing the discipline of its experiences, but by dealing with them in the best possible manner, maintaining a calm and steadfast mind, a quiet faith and an unflinching spirit.

July 30th

Prentice Mulford

Your prevailing mood, or frame of mind, has more to do than anything else with your success or failure in any undertaking. Your mind is that amount of thought-substance which has come together during countless ages, and after using many physical bodies. The mind is a magnet. It has the power, first of attracting thought, and next of sending that thought out again. You do not, of yourself, make your thought: you only receive and feel it as it comes to you. What kind of thought you most charge that magnet (your mind) with, or set it open to receive, it will attract most of that kind to you. If, then, you think, or keep most in mind, the mere thought of determination, hope, cheerfulness, strength, force, power, justice, gentleness, order, and precision, you will attract and receive more and more of such thought-elements. These are among the elements of success. These qualities are of thought-element as real things as any we see or feel. The more you set the magnet in this direction, the stronger it grows to attract these elements. Whatever of thought you think or receive, you send from you again, an invisible substance to act on others. Your own thought is now in the air, acting on and attracting to you of its kind the thought of others, whose bodies you may never have seen. The people you are in the future to meet, who may help or damage your fortunes, are those whose thought in like manner sent far from their bodies has already met and mingled with your own. That attraction tends to bring you together in the body. It will certainly bring you together in some form of existence.

July 31st

Orison Swett Marden

Why not begin now to make the unseen forces your friends? Instead of making them your enemies, why not turn about face mentally and work with the law by simply holding the right thought? Why not turn your back on disease and poverty and failure by continually holding the health and abundance thought, saying to yourself: "I AM the child of the Author of health, joy, and abundance; I AM the child of the All-Supply. Health and success continually flow to me from the All-Supply, which is the Source of my being. Nothing but myself can cut me off from this Source; nothing but my own wrong thinking can cut off my supply, — the health, success, and happiness that are my birthright. I claim my inheritance from my Father now. I AM health; I AM success; I AM happiness; I AM free now and forever from all that would hinder my development, from everything that would hinder the realization of the ambitions the Father himself has implanted in me. This is my appointed work, the task he has given me to do here on this earth — to carry out the details of his plan for me is to realize my ambitions. I AM working in partnership with Him and I cannot fail. I AM one with Him; I again make my affirmation: I AM health; I AM success; I AM happiness; I AM abundance. My future is secure. I will go straight on, fearing nothing, for there is nothing to fear when I know that God is all, and that I AM one with Him.'" No matter what your present circumstances and environment, if you hold fast to this mental attitude, to a firm belief in the reality of the unseen, where your supply is, and work in harmony with the law, you can, through the creative power of thought, acting on the invisible universal substance, fashion and draw out of the unseen realms of supply whatever you will — knowledge, wisdom, power, health, wealth, happiness, success, — the realization of all your hopes and visions.

August

August 1st

Ernest Holmes

When we look into the mental reason for things we find out why things happen. The man who gets so far and never seems to go beyond that point is still governed by law; when he allows his thoughts to take him out into larger fields of action, his conditions come up to his thought; when he stops enlarging his thought he stops growing. If he would still keep on in thought, realizing more and still more, he would find that in the outer form of things he would be doing greater things. There are many reasons why a man stops thinking larger things. One of them is a lack of imagination. He cannot conceive of anything more to follow than that which has already happened. Another thought works like this: "This is as far as anyone can go in my business." Right here he signs his own death warrant. Often a person will say, "I am too old to do bigger things." There he stops. Someone else will say, "Competition is too great"; and here is where this man stops; he can go no further than his thought will carry him.

August 2nd

Joseph Murphy

Perhaps you are saying as you read this chapter, "I need wealth and success." This is what you do: Repeat for about five minutes to yourself three or four times a day, Wealth — Success. These words have tremendous power. They represent the inner power of the subconscious mind. Anchor your mind on this substantial power within you; then conditions and circumstances corresponding to their nature and quality will be manifested in your life. You are not saying, "I AM wealthy," you are dwelling on real powers within you. There is no conflict in the mind when you say, —Wealth.‖ Furthermore, the feeling of wealth will well up within you as you dwell on the idea of wealth. The feeling of wealth produces wealth; keep this in mind at all times. Your subconscious mind is like a bank, a sort of universal financial institution. It magnifies whatever you deposit or impress upon it whether it is the idea of wealth or of poverty. Choose wealth.

August 3rd

Christian Larson

The work you do, be it with mind or muscle, invariably conveys the spirit of your own soul. Therefore work in the spirit of joy and your work will be the product of joy, a rare product the best of its kind. It is the man who blends rejoicing with his work who does the best work; it is the man who deeply and sincerely enjoys his work who gives the greatest worth to his work; and the more worth we give to our work the more of the rich and the worthy our work will bring to us. We realize therefore that it is profitable in every way to learn to be glad. But it is not only profitable to ourselves; also to all others that we may reach through word or deed. Then the profit that comes from the art of being glad is never the result of selfishness. The glad heart is never selfish. The sunbeam does not dance and sing to please its own restricted desire; it does what it does because it is what it is a happy, carefree sunbeam. It is the same with the glad heart, it sings because it has become the spirit of song; and all are charmed with the song.

August 4th

James Allen

Man is subject to the law of habit. Is he then free? Yes, he is free. Man did not make life and its laws; they are eternal; he finds himself involved in them and he can understand and obey them. Man's power does not enable him to make laws of being; it subsists in discrimination and choice. Man does not create one jot of the universal conditions or laws; they are the essential principles of things, and are neither made nor unmade. He discovers, not makes, them. Ignorance of them is at the root of the world's pain. To defy them is folly and bondage. Who is the freer man, the thief who defies the laws of his country or the honest citizen who obeys them? Who, again, is the freer man, the fool who thinks he can live as he likes, or the wise man who chooses to do only that which is right?

August 5th

Ernest Holmes

Man's word, spoken forth into creative mind, is endowed with power of expression. "By our words we are justified and by our words we are condemned." Our word has the exact amount of power that we put into it. This does not mean power through effort or strain but power through absolute conviction, or faith. It is like a little messenger who knows what he is doing and knows just how to do it. We speak into our words the intelligence which we are, and backed by that greater intelligence of the Universal Mind our word becomes a law unto the thing for which it is spoken. Jesus understood this far better than we do. Indeed, He absolutely believed it, for He said, "Heaven and earth shall pass away but my words shall not pass away till all be fulfilled." This makes our word inseparable from Absolute Intelligence and Power. Now if any word has power it must follow that all words have power. Some words may have a greater power than others, according to our conviction, but all words have some power. How careful, then, we should be what kind of words we are speaking.

August 6th

Uriel Buchanan

By the thought you are holding today, you are shaping the future, for good or ill. If you have in your mind an image of a bright and prosperous future, if you see yourself in better surroundings, with greater ability and better opportunities for advancement, if you see yourself as being successful in all undertakings, you are using a thought force which will result in the constant improvement of material conditions. Men who are the most' prosperous live in a thought atmosphere of cheerfulness. They are always confident, hopeful and determined. You should carefully avoid the thought atmosphere of the discouraged and despondent. The influence of their negative, confused thoughts will cause depression, unrest and fear. If you are daily associated with people who are unhealthy, avaricious and sordid, who live in the belief of the material and perishable, you will be affected more or less by similar influences. It is very difficult to realize the positive condition of mind which is permanently freed from periods of depression, while associating with people who are continually sending out anxious, worried and discordant thoughts. But clearness and brilliancy of mind, and health and strength of body, will generate a silent power which will be far more potent than any destructive influence; and every undesirable thought force, coming from immature minds, can be readily turned into a higher, better channel.

August 7th

Robert Collier

There are more riches in this old earth than mankind can ever exhaust. There is more power in the atom alone than man can ever use. There are unlimited resources of food and riches and comfort as yet undreamed of by man. Why then do so many live in squalor, even in this richest country in the world? Why do millions die of famine in India and China? For the same reason that a party of explorers, driven by a west wind from the Amazon River far out to sea, and drifting in a river of fresh water, they almost perished of thirst! In much the same way, millions of human beings, living in a world of plenty, perish of want. God is not partial to a fortunate few. He does not give to them and let the rest starve. He gives freely to all! But there are certain laws governing these riches of His. There are rules that must be complied with. And until you learn the rules, you are like Ali Baba without the magic "Open, Sesame!" to open the doors of the treasure trove. You have heard of Einstein's "Law of Relativity." And you probably wondered at times why such a to-do should be made over an obscure scientific law that could have no bearing, as far as you could see, upon everyday life. But do you know that Einstein's theory is as important to you as any law in the land? For on what is his theory based? 1st, that there is only one material in the Universe. 2nd, and this is the part with a direct bearing upon you — that there is only one fundamental Law of the Universe. That law is the Law of Attraction. Perhaps you will get the connection more readily if I give you this law as it is expressed in the Bible. There it reads "To him that hath shall be given, and from him that hath not, shall be taken away even that which he hath." To put it in ordinary, everyday language Einstein's Law of the Universe and the Biblical precept both mean that you must either be an Attracter, drawing things to you, or else be willing to sit back and see everything that is yours attracted to some stronger personality.

August 8th

Venice J. Bloodworth

You have learned to ignore appearance; now still more important is the fact that you must guard your thoughts diligently and keep your mind on a hopeful, happy plane. Keep yourself in a successful frame of mind because you receive subconsciously thoughts and ideas that correspond to your own state of mind. We "key in" on each other's thoughts like the radio, and receive "wireless" messages continuously. Therefore, you can readily grasp the fact that if your thoughts are blue and discouraged, you will receive thoughts of poverty, disease, and distress; on the other hand, if your mind is clear, hopeful, and happy, you will receive the best thoughts from the best minds, and ideas thus received are sometimes very valuable.

August 9th

Ernest Holmes

"Resist not evil and it will flee from you." Here is a statement of one of the great laws of our being. When we resist we make a mental image of the thing we are fighting, and that tends to have it created for us. When we learn to look only at what we want and never at what we do not want, we will no longer resist anything. "Suffer it to be so now." You need not try to change the world. Let it alone; all people are doing the best they can. No one needs to be saved but yourself, and the sooner you realize this the sooner you will attain. Get over that "holier than thou" attitude. It is an illusion that many people suffer from, especially in the religious world. The world is all right; it is not going to Hell; it is on the way to Heaven. It is getting good so fast that in the process many things are being overturned and confusion appears to be on the surface. A great change is taking place, and on the surface the results are as yet a little mixed, but underneath, the power is at work destroying all unlike itself. In time all will come to see this. What a load of responsibility we assume that we were never meant to carry.

August 10th

Eugene Del Mar

Man has been provided with a wonderful instrument whereby he may create and possess the objects of his desire. He has potential powers that have hardly been stirred into activity. He has unsuspected depths of energy that have barely been tapped. Why is it that ages have been permitted to pass by, and these powers and energies been practically neglected? What is the hidden wonder that might revolutionize the life of man? Why has it not already fulfilled its purpose? Can it be that man has knowledge of this instrument, and yet permits it to remain undeveloped? The existence of an instrument having such tremendous powers cannot but be admitted. The only question unsettled is as to the extent to which these powers may be exercised. The instrument has been used from time immemorial, and the powers have been exercised to some extent; but man has never understood their real significance or the grandeur of his creative abilities. A vast difference between the present age and the preceding ones is that a larger degree of intelligence has become more widely diffused, and the knowledge and wisdom of the few have become the property of the many. Some of the mysteries and miracles of bygone ages are now mere common-places, and children prattle of many things that wise men formerly regarded as treasures of wisdom. In that respect, and particularly in relation to material and physical matters, the world has made tremendous strides. It has acquired vast stores of knowledge, albeit its stock of wisdom has not increased proportionately.

Rather has modern knowledge been used to buttress and support ancient wisdom, thereby opening up the avenues of its appropriation to the average intellect. What has been the instrument of this transformation whereby "the man of the street" has gained access to knowledge and wisdom that formerly was monopolized by the few wise of bygone days? There is but one possible answer to this question; but one instrument that could have achieved such tremendous results. The human mind has been the instrument; and the Freedom of the Universe is accorded to man to the degree that he gives freedom to his thought.

August 11th

Joseph Murphy

When you are seeking to convey the idea of wealth and success to your subconscious mind, be sure you never make foolish statements, such as: "I despise money." "It is an evil thing." "It is the root of all evil." Such an attitude of mind will cause money to take wings and fly away from you. You would then be giving two conflicting orders to the subconscious mind; one would neutralize the other, and nothing would happen. Money has taken many forms down through the ages. What you really want is to have a subconscious conviction that money will always be in constant circulation in your life, meeting all of your needs at every moment of time and every point of space.

August 12th

Orison Swett Marden

We often wonder why it is that certain people, in apparently no better circumstances than we are, get so much better things than we do; why they always insist upon and receive the best of everything. We never see them wearing cheap things — never see cheap things in their homes, or any pinching anywhere. They buy the best food, the best fruits and vegetables in the market, and everything else in accordance. We think they are extravagant when we compare what they pay for things with what we pay for things of the same kind, and we pride ourselves that we are economizing and saving what they are wasting. But, are we? How does our manner of living compare with theirs? Does the enjoyment we get out of life measure up to what they get? Do the few dollars we save compensate for the great lack in our lives — the lack of good food, of proper clothing, of the little pleasure trips, the social enjoyments, the picnics and various diversions which make life pleasant, healthful, and above all, much more productive for the neighbors whose extravagance we condemn? As a matter of fact, our skimped, pinching policy leaves us poorer in the end.

August 13th

Ernest Holmes

The secret place of the Most High is in his own soul, where God dwells in eternal peace and infinite calm. Here he walks the waters of life undisturbed by the waves and the storm. Divine companionship is his for all eternity. Peace which transcends all human confusion comes, and he realizes that indeed he is honored of the Father. His word is flung out and will work and none can hinder it; the sense of sureness is complete. Heaven and earth may pass away, but the word goes on and on accomplishing that thing for which it was sent; and all power is given to it on earth and in heaven. If he speaks to the sick and they receive, it will heal them. If he says the word of prosperity it will manifest, and nothing can hinder it; the world will abound with good, and his cup run over with life.

August 14th

Prentice Mulford

Do not waste your power in looking for such aiding forces with your body. Let silent, persistent resolve in mind do the work. It will do it if you persevere holding to this frame of mind. It is no new power, though possibly new to most of us. It is constantly, though unconsciously, exercised for good or ill all about us. Because your body is not the only power you have to work with. Your body is only the instrument used by your mind, or spirit. Your mind, your invisible self, uses your body in, say, cutting down a tree, or other work of hand, exactly as your body uses the axe. But when such force (thought) is not using the body, it is at work with greater power elsewhere. To think persistent resolve, to think persistent push in your one aim and purpose, — to simply think it, and do nothing else, — will create for you a power as certain to move and effect results as the jackscrews placed under the heaviest building will move it upward. The power you so create of your mind and of unseen forces will work while you sleep. It will bring to you new devices, plans, and methods for moving your business forward. And as you get these plans, they will move your body to act. You cannot sit still when an idea that means business comes to you: such idea is for you power. But you can tire your body to such an extent that you will have no power to receive an idea when it does come. All successful business is based on a continual inflowing of new idea, plan, device, scheme.

August 15th

Floyd B. Wilson

It may seem to many of the readers of this paper that I have gone over-minutely into detail in placing before them the meaning of this simple word, thought. However, I have done this because as I go forward in the series of papers I am asked to write, over and over again I will need to refer to the power of thought, and I wish to give a clear idea of my understanding and particular use of the word. Man may discipline himself to control his own thoughts. These, properly fashioned and planted in his subconsciousness, will generate and grow. From time to time he may change the course of his thinking, and when he does this he will change his personality, ascending or descending according as he wills. How to master the thought machinery to meet one's desire is not so difficult as it may appear to be to those unacquainted with true mental discipline. First, it is necessary to bring one's self to a complete recognition of the mighty force which is developed by right thinking; and, second, having learned this, to sow the carefully culled thought seeds which by an inevitable law produce their kind, and the harvest will then always be the ripe, golden fruit of desire.

August 16th

Christian Larson

The creative power of the mind works through a certain law; a law that we may well designate as the great law in human life. It is the law that determines what we are to accomplish, what we are to become, and what the future is to be. And the reason for this can be simply explained. The sum-total of what we are, and what we have — all the issues of life, in fact — these things are the result of what the creative power of the mind is doing; and the great law determines what the creative power is to do, in us and for us; in what direction it is to act; what it is to form, produce and create, and to what extent. The great law is this: what we place deeply in the mind, this creative power will work for. What we place deeply in the mind — in the form of a thought, image, picture or impression — this power will produce, develop, create, bring forth or enlarge upon; and these things are sometimes enlarged upon enormously. And, also, what is already in the mind — in the form of habit, instinct or fixed belief — this power will continue to work for, perpetuate and bring forth. What you place deeply in the mind, is received by this power as your "word" of instruction as to what you want done. If you place something there that is good — a good thought or a good idea — this power will work for that idea, and give it increasing life, action and expression. But if you place something there that is imperfect, wrong or detrimental, this power will work for that, and produce the wrong and the detrimental in your life.

August 17th

Ernest Holmes

Never get away from the fact that you are surrounded by such a power; it is the principle of demonstration. It knows every thought. As we send forth our thought into it, it does unto us. The person who is ignorant of this law must by that ignorance be bound by his thought, by his human beliefs. One who understands will begin to break these ties that bind him; one by one he will destroy every negative thought until at last he is able to think what he wants to think; and so he frees himself by the use of the same power that at one time bound him. We must destroy all thought that we would not see manifest and hold to that which we would see, until we receive the affirmative answer.

August 18th

James Allen

There can be no progress, no achievement without sacrifice. A man's worldly success will be in the measure that he sacrifices his confused animal thoughts, and fixes his mind on the development of his plans, and the strengthening of his resolution and self reliance. And the higher he lifts his thoughts, the more manly, upright, and righteous he becomes, the greater will be his success, the more blessed an enduring will be his achievements. The universe does not favor the greedy, the dishonest, the vicious, although on the mere surface it may sometimes appear to do so; it helps the honest, the magnanimous, the virtuous. All the great Teachers of the ages have declared this in varying forms, and to prove and know it a man has but to persist in making himself more and more virtuous by lifting up his thoughts.

August 19th

Joseph Murphy

Regardless of what kind of news you received today, you could go to the mirror, look at your face, lips, eyes, and your gestures, as you tell yourself and imagine you have heard the news of having received a vast fortune. Dramatize it, feel it, thrill to it, and notice how your whole body responds to the inner thrill. You can reverse any situation through prayer. Busy your mind with the concepts of peace, success, wealth, and happiness. Identify yourself with these ideas mentally, emotionally, and pictorially. Get a picture of yourself as you want to be; retain that image; sustain it with joy, faith, and expectancy; finally you will succeed in experiencing its manifestation.

August 20th

Henry Thomas Hamblin

It is a proved scientific fact that you grow into the likeness of that upon which you meditate. If you meditate upon evil then evil will come into your life; if you meditate upon revenge, your life will be turned into an inferno of trouble; on the other hand, if you meditate upon happiness and other higher mental states, then happiness will be yours, and if you let your thoughts dwell upon "peace" then peace of mind will result. All these states and many others are within you; they can be called forth by meditation. You can call forth either good or evil, success or failure, strength or weakness, happiness or woe, everything is in your own hands. It will be helpful for you to think of your subliminal Mind as another person, one who is always listening, listening, listening. He hears all that you say, and ACTS UPON all the thoughts that you let pass the threshold of the inner mind. "Hush! he is listening," should be the watch-word of your life. Let no thought of evil, of impurity, of weakness, of ill-health, of failure, of hate, of anger, of fear, enter your Subliminal Mind, for he will receive them as orders which he will obey, and being all-powerful, great and terrible will be the results. Therefore let only thoughts of good, purity, strength, health, success, love, self-control, courage and determination enter this greater mind of vast intelligence and power. Do this, and your Subliminal Mind will take these thoughts as orders, and will shape your life and health accordingly. Thus in a general way your Subliminal Mind will be led to develop your life on healthful and successful, noble and harmonious lines. Let "Hush! he is listening" be the watch-word of your life.

August 21st

Ernest Holmes

Man must know that the Spirit not only can manifest through him, but that it wishes to do so; "The Father seeks such to worship Him." The practitioner who understands the truth knows that as long as God exists, he will exist; that he could no more become non-existent than God could. Walking, talking, moving in God, he must not only see the Divine Being as the great unknown Cause, but he must go a step further and see God as the great self-knowing, understanding power of Infinite Intelligence, thinking through his own thought and willing into his own life all power and all good. More than this, God must become within his own soul the greater self, the inner life, the inner light that is to light his path with sure step to the attainment of the greater ideals. God is to become the great friend of his life, understanding him, and helping him at all times to understand all things.

August 22nd

Uriel Buchanan

Desire is the invincible magnet which establishes an affinity with the objective world and draws from environment the things most desired. The direction of desire determines the course of man's destiny. If man desires only the true and the good, he has power to gradually surround himself with associations kindred to his yearnings; or if he desires the frivolities of life and is governed by ignoble thoughts which arise from the lower instincts, he will attract failure and misfortune. When there is intense concentration of thought by one deeply in earnest, a magnetic battery is formed in the vital centers which imparts to the body a positive vibration that acts on other persons and compels response, influencing all who are brought within range. He who once feels this power awakening within realizes to what heights he may ascend and receives a foregleam of the possibilities which await him. To come into a realization of power you must cultivate a true love for the highest ideas of the mind. The degree of love's intensity will determine the force of the heart's desire; and desire is the magic wand which kindles the hidden fire of the will and awakens the resolve to do and dare. You must learn patience and silence, and weave the elements of your being into a chord of harmony and strength. Conserve the forces which nature has given you and direct them by an invincible will to the highest uses of life.

August 23rd

Robert Collier

To man has been given the job of emulating his Maker — of becoming a creator, finding new and broader and better ways through which to express the Creative Force in him. His is the work of creating beauty, or bringing more of comfort, of joy and happiness into the world. To every living thing on earth is given a measure of Creative Power. Of the lower forms of life all that is required is that they bring forth fruit according to their kind — "some thirty, some sixty, some an hundred fold." Of you, however, much more is expected. To bring forth fruit according to your physical kind is good — but that is no more than the animals do. More is required of you. You must bring forth fruit, according to your mental kind as well! You are a son of God, a creator. Therefore creation is expected of you. You are to spread seeds not merely of human kind, but of the intellect as well. You are to leave the world a better place than you found it, with more of joy in it, more of beauty, of comfort, of understanding, of light.

August 24th

Venice J. Bloodworth

You are using your creative power of thought every minute; the problem is to use it consciously and correctly, thus creating only desirable results. Cheerful, happy, constructive, loving, kindly thoughts set in motion vibrations which bring us good results. Thoughts of worry, envy, hatred, criticism and other thoughts of discord set in motion vibrations that bring bad results. Every cell in your body is intelligent and will respond to your direction and will create the exact pattern you give it. Therefore if you place a perfect ideal before the subconscious mind, its creative energies will build a perfect body. So if you wish to manifest health, your predominant mental attitude must be one of health, strength and vigor. All the elements of nature are pure. All the forces of existence are harmonious. But man, the supreme ruler in the realm of effect, may take the perfections of Being and through his thinking processes build a world of sickness and distress. We have educated our faculties to believe inharmonious conditions real until it has become a fixed belief in the race mind that sickness, poverty and discord are necessary. Some people believe that trials are a punishment for what we call our sins. It is true that we find many appearances of evil, but these conditions were brought about through ignorance and a belief in evil as a principle acting in opposition to good. We have not stopped to reason about this because we are so used to accepting the evidence of our senses without question.

August 25th

Ernest Holmes

The way that we are using mind through our thought is the way that we are treating ourselves for prosperity. So simple, and yet we have not understood it! If a man says, "I have not." he will not receive; if he says, "I have," he will receive. "To those who have shall be given, and to those who have not shall be taken away even that which they have." This is a veiled statement of the law of cause and effect. When you send out into mind the thought that you have not, it accepts the idea and takes away from you even that which you have. Reverse the process and say, "I have," and it will at once set to work to create for you even more than you now possess. You will readily see then that you are not dealing with two powers but with one, and that it operates through your own thought, doing unto all even as they believe.

August 26th

Orison Swett Marden

While the subconscious mind is all-powerful in working out the pattern or idea we give it, of itself it does not originate, so it will make all the difference in the world to you what sort of material you give your subconscious mind to work on. You can make it an enemy or a friend, for it will do the thing which injures you just as quickly as the thing which blesses you. Not through malice, but because it has no discriminating power any more than the soil in which the farmer sows his seed. If the farmer should make a mistake and sow thistle seed instead of wheat, the soil doesn't say to him, "My friend, you have made a mistake. You have been sowing thistle seed instead of wheat, so we will change the law, which you may get what you thought you were going to get." No, the soil will always give us a harvest like our sowing. If we sow thistle seed it will be just as faithful in producing thistles as it will in producing wheat or cabbages or potatoes. We sow the seed and nature gives us a corresponding harvest; that is the law on the physical plane. It is exactly the same on the mental plane. The subconscious mind is like the soil, passive. The objective mind uses it, gives its commands or suggestions, which it carries out according to their nature. That is, the objective or conscious mind sows the seed in word, motive, thought or act, and the subconscious mind gives us back our own; always the thing that corresponds to what we impressed on it. In other words, the subconscious mind has no choice but to follow the lead we give it. Hence, how important it is that our instructions to this invisible servant should be for our good and not for our harm; that we should saturate it, not with the things we do not want, the things we hate and fear and worry about, but the things we long for and are striving to attain.

August 27th

Christian Larson

The purpose of life is continuous advancement, and this necessitates the constant appropriation of the new, and the constant elimination of the old. To promote the first essential, a practical system of ideals is required; and to promote the second, we must master the art of letting go. If we desire the new to be created, the creative process of mind must be supplied with new and better impressions. Should we fail to do this, the creative energies will employ the old ideas, or impressions that are suggested from without. In the mastery of fate, one of the greatest essentials is to prevent environment from impressing the mind; and to prevent this, your mind should be filled with your own ideal impressions. But this is not possible to any satisfactory degree unless a definite system of idealism is adopted, because no impression will become strong and predominant unless it is given constant attention. In this connection, the true use of the imagination becomes extremely important. Everything that we imagine we impress upon mind; therefore, through the imagination we can work ourselves into almost any condition or state of being. In meeting circumstances and events imagination can be made to serve a most valuable service, and thus become directly instrumental in changing environment and fate. When adversity comes we usually try to find the silver lining; but when we fail to find this, discouragement follows, which in turn but intensifies the darkness and the trouble. However, we can create a silver lining with the imagination that will serve the same purpose; because when we picture the better side of things, and keep mind steadily upon that picture, the better will impress itself upon the mind. The result is that our thoughts change for the better, and we improve with our thoughts; and the improvement of man means the improvement of his environment. Anyone who is in trouble can work himself out by creating in his imagination the silver lining of emancipation, and keeping the eye single upon that ideal picture.

August 28th

Joseph Murphy

Pick up the paper any day, and you can read dozens of items that could sow the seeds of futility, fear, worry, anxiety, and impending doom. If accepted by you, these thoughts of fear could cause you to lose the will for life. Knowing that you can reject all these negative suggestions by giving your subconscious mind constructive autosuggestions, you counteract all these destructive ideas. Check regularly on the negative suggestions that people make to you. You do not have to be influenced by destructive heterosuggestion. All of us have suffered from it in our childhood and in our teens. If you look back, you can easily recall how parents, friends, relatives, teachers, and associates contributed in a campaign of negative suggestions. Study the things said to you, and you will discover much of it was in the form of propaganda. The purpose of much of what was said was to control you or instill fear into you. This heterosuggestion process goes on in every home, office, factory, and club. You will find that many of these suggestions are for the purpose of making you think, feel, and act, as others want you to and in ways that are to their advantage.

August 29th

Eugene Del Mar

Without the mask Man would be invisible; but without the Man there could be no mask. The Man creates his mask, wears it, changes it, and finally discards it. But the Man never changes. The mask is the clothing, the home, the residence of the Man, which he is forever patching and altering to suit his changing fancy. It may seem that the Man is changing, but it is only his covering that is being fashioned differently to meet his changing thought seasons. As Man is a deathless Soul, identified with Universal Spirit, one can do little or nothing for Man himself. But the mask is Man's creation, and, being impermanent, ever-changing, illusive, and delusive, it is that which requires his never-ceasing attention. It is as the mask is guided by strong and controlled emotions, and by clear and definite thought, that the Soul qualities are realized, and Man enters on the enjoyment of self-revelation. The profoundest study for man is Man, and his deepest satisfaction is to watch his own self-revelation; after seeing himself as a worm or caterpillar, crawling on the earth, to witness his gradual metamorphosis into a butterfly or Spiritual Being, with gorgeous habiliments, disclosing from beneath his disguise the indisputable proofs of his divine origin. This is the Man behind the mask, a Being of infinite glory, but environed by forests of ignorance that obscure his vision, by rivers of doubt that benumb his faculties, and by clouds of fear that stifle his energies. Ignorance, doubt, and fear were the principal factors that served to fashion his mask, but these are merely the primitive aspects of wisdom, faith, and courage.

August 30th

Ernest Holmes

You are going to establish in your rooms such an atmosphere of success that it will become an irresistible power; it will sweep everything before it as it realizes the greatness and the All-Mightiness of the One. You are so sure, that you will not even look to see if it is going to happen; you KNOW. And now your word, which is one with the Infinite Life, is to be spoken in calm, perfect trust. It is to be taken up, and at once it is to be operated on. Perfect is the pattern and perfect will be the result. You see yourself surrounded by the thing that you desire. More than this, you are the thing that you desire. Your word is now establishing it forever; see this, feel it, know it. You are now encompassed by perfect life, by infinite activity, by all power, by all guidance. The power of the Spirit is drawing to you all people; it is supplying you with all good; it is filling you with all life, truth and love. Wait in perfect silence while that inner power takes it up. And then you know that it is done unto you. There goes forth from this word the power of the Infinite. "The words which I speak, they are spirit and they are life."

August 31st

Henry Thomas Hamblin

There must be a purpose in life, and this must have for its object the betterment of the lives of others, either few or many. The law of service must be obeyed, otherwise there can be no happiness. This may fill some readers with dismay, for they may be employed in an occupation that apparently does no good to anybody. They may feel that if they were engaged in some noble enterprise for the uplift of humanity, then they could truly serve, but in their present occupation this is impossible. To think thus is very natural, yet the truth is we can all obey the law of service, and can begin now, in our present occupation, no matter what it may be. We have only to do our daily work, not as a task which must be 'got through,' in order to bring us a living, or because it is expected of us that we should work, but as an offering of love to life and the world, in order to come into harmony with the great law of service. Our ideas of values with regard to occupations are altogether erroneous, from the 'inner wisdom' point of view. The scrubbing of a doorstep, if faithfully done in a true spirit of service, is of as much value and real importance as the writing of a deathless poem, or dying for one's country. We can never truthfully say that one act of service is of greater value, or is more important than another. All that the higher law looks at is the motive. Therefore, if your motive is right, you can be engaged in the humblest and, apparently, most useless occupation, and yet be happy because you satisfy the law of service.

September

The Within Creates The Without: Daily Meditations

September 1st

Robert Collier

Every condition, every experience of life is the result of our mental attitude. We can do only what we think we can do. We can be only what we think we can be. We can have only what we think we can have. What we do, what we are, what we have, all depend upon what we think. We can never express anything that we do not first have in mind. The secret of all power, all success, all riches, is in first thinking powerful thoughts, successful thoughts, thoughts of wealth and supply. We must build them in our minds first. "Could we rightly comprehend the mind of man," wrote Paracelsus, "nothing would be impossible to us upon the earth." And Buddha told his followers — "All that we are is the result of what we have thought." And thought is subject wholly to the control of mind. Its direction rests with us. So learn to control your thought. Learn to image upon your mind only things you want to see reflected in your outer circumstances. Our achievements of today are but the sum of our thoughts of yesterday. Remember, you can have anything you want if you want it badly enough. You can be anything you want to be, have anything you desire, accomplish anything you set out to accomplish — if you will hold to that desire with singleness of purpose; if you will understand and believe in your own powers to accomplish.

September 2nd

Venice J. Bloodworth

Your mind and its present state of development controls the materialization of the Universal Mind through you. Your present subconscious impressions determine exactly what you are now. So please do not jump to the conclusion that you can read the truth set forth herein and go right out and start manifesting an entirely new set of conditions. An acorn is the seed of a mighty oak, but the law of growth must unfold and build up the tree. And while the Holy Spirit within you is not subject to time in the same way that a tree must be, you must gain understanding through meditation and study, for a new consciousness must be developed before a new set of conditions can arise. A person who has thought in limited terms cannot, at first, picture himself possessing and using a huge amount of money; but he can see himself spending wisely a reasonable amount and can gradually entertain the idea of a million dollars. To keep your equilibrium, your consciousness must change first, causing new ideas, which in turn makes new and larger demands on your subconscious mind. These demands will be met in perfect accord with the unseen pattern or mental picture held by you.

September 3rd

Ernest Holmes

One single stream of thought, daily sent out into Creative Mind, will do wonders. Within a year the person who will practice this will have completely changed his conditions of life. The way to practice this is daily to spend some time in thinking and in mentally seeing just what is wanted; see the thing just as it is wished and then affirm that this is now done. Try to feel that what has been stated is the truth. Words and affirmations simply give shape to thought; they are not creative. Feeling is creative and the more feeling that is put into the word the greater power it will have over conditions. In doing this we think of the condition only as an effect, something that follows what we think. It cannot help following our thought. This is the way that all creation comes into expression.

September 4th

Joseph Murphy

If you think negatively, destructively, and viciously, these thoughts generate destructive emotions which must be expressed and find an outlet. These emotions, being of a negative nature, are frequently expressed as ulcers, heart trouble, tension, and anxieties. What is your idea or feeling about yourself now? Every part of your being expresses that idea. Your vitality, body, financial status, friends, and social status represent a perfect reflection of the idea you have of yourself. This is the real meaning of what is impressed in your subconscious mind, and which is expressed in all phases of your life. We injure ourselves by the negative ideas, which we entertain. How often have you wounded yourself by getting angry, fearful, jealous, or vengeful? These are the poisons that enter your subconscious mind. You were not born with these negative attitudes. Feed your subconscious mind life-giving thoughts, and you will wipe out all the negative patterns lodged therein. As you continue to do this, all the past will be wiped out and remembered no more.

September 5th

James Allen

The outer world of circumstance shapes itself to the inner world of thought, and both pleasant and unpleasant external conditions are factors which make for the ultimate good of the individual. As the reaper of his own harvest, man learns both by suffering and bliss. A man does not come to the almshouse or the jail by the tyranny of fate of circumstance, but by the pathway of groveling thoughts and base desires. Nor does a pure-minded man fall suddenly into crime by stress of any mere external force; the criminal thought had long been secretly fostered in the heart, and the hour of opportunity revealed its gathered power.

September 6th

Prentice Mulford

There are certain general laws; but every individual must apply the general law to him or herself. It is a general law that the wind will propel a ship. But every vessel does not use the air in exactly the same fashion. It is a general law that thought is force, and can effect, and is constantly effecting, results to others far from our bodies; and the quality of our thought and its power to affect results depends very much on our associations. But for that reason, if yours is the superior thought or power, and I see that through its use you are moving ahead in the world, I should not choose your character of associates or your manner of life. I can try your methods as experiments; but I must remember they are only experiments. I must avoid that so common error, – the error of slavish copy and idolatry of another.

September 7th

Ernest Holmes

The way can be shown, but each individual must himself walk the way. We are so bound by suggestion and hypnotized by false belief, so entangled by the chaotic thinking of the world, thinking which is based upon the principle of a dual mind, that we become confused and are not ourselves. Wake up! Your word is all-powerful, your consciousness is one with Omnipotence. Your thought is infinite. Your destiny is eternal and your home is everlasting heaven. Realize the truth . . I AM living in a perfect universe, it always was perfect and always will be perfect. There never was a mistake made, there are no mistakes being made, and there never will be. I live in the great and eternal universe of perfection from cause to effect, from beginning to end, and "The world's all right, and I know it."

September 8th

George Schubel

We can say of the thought-image what the photographer is able to say of his light-image, that it is on its way toward the first stage of its outward tangible materialization or reproduction as a mental photograph, and when we understand this consciously and fully, then all doubt about the reality of the mental-photographic process will cease. We have only to consider the fact that the photographer's film has impressed upon it nothing more than a collection of light-rays, nothing more than a light-image offset by a shadow, and which is altogether invisible to the sense-sight, yet when he subsequently applies the appropriate developing process to it, he finds that that which for the moment is invisible on the sensitive surface of the photographic film gradually formulates itself into that which is visible to the eye. It is a marvelous fact yet perfectly natural in both instances, and that which is true of the photographic film is just as true of the subjective impressionable element of the mind of which the film is the outward chemicalized correspondent. Our heart's desire forms itself into that which is but a thought at first; the thought becomes projected and impressed upon our subjective thinking and by the process of development becomes the thing which is visible to our eyes.

September 9th

Uriel Buchanan

Man knows that the myriad forms of nature are expressions of the Infinite Mind and that he may attract from them a part and quality of the Infinite. The earth and all it contains, the melody of the winds and waters, the grandeur of the woods and plains, and the beauty of all living things, speak with a pleading eloquence which bids man arise in the dignity of the power that nature has given him, and to manifest the growing harmonies that spring up from within. To grow in wisdom, to have a lighter heart and greater freedom, to commence each day with the feeling of a new pleasure, a higher hope and more determined endeavor, we must draw nearer to the Infinite and absorb the element of life and power from the trees and plants and all the myriad expressions of nature. The closer we feel our relationship with nature, the more can we attract of the qualities of the Supreme Mind pervading all things. And the more refined we become, the greater will be our power to appreciate the indescribable beauty and harmony of the rugged mountains, the forests and valleys.

September 10th

Christian Larson

If the principle of self-supremacy did not exist, man could not exercise complete control over anything at any time; but every mind demonstrates supremacy many times every hour. The mastership exercised over mind and body in various ways may be confined to limited spheres of action; but within those spheres of action the mastership is complete. And those spheres will expand constantly as the principle of self-supremacy is applied on a larger and a larger scale. Since the principle of complete control exists in man, there is a way to apply that principle in everything, and at all times. But to accomplish this, the attitude of self-supremacy must prevail at all times, and under all conditions. While man is in the attitude of self-supremacy, he exercises complete control over certain things in his life; but when he enters the belief that he is controlled or influenced by other things, he leaves the attitude of self-supremacy, and ceases to exercise his complete control. In the present state of human development, the average mind is so constituted that it oscillates from one state to another, remaining the greater part of the time in the attitude of self-submission; due principally to the fact that we are seldom absolutely true to the higher conviction, and also because we try to think that both beliefs are true at the same time. Consequently, the great essential for man in his present state is to accept the high conviction as an absolute truth, and be true to that truth every moment of existence. To be true to that truth he must refuse absolutely to believe that he can be controlled or influenced by anything or anybody. He must depart completely from the belief in the control of other powers, and must recognize in himself the only power to control the power to control completely, everything in his own domain.

September 11th

Ernest Holmes

When Jesus said, "All things whatsoever ye pray and ask for, believe that ye receive them and ye shall have them," he was uttering one of those many deep truths that were so clear to Him and that we are just beginning to see. He knew that everything is made out of mind and that without that positive acceptance on the part of the individual there is no mold into which mind can pour itself forth into form. In the mind of God there is the correct mold, the true knowing, but in the mind of man there is not always this true knowing. Since God can do for us only by doing through us, nothing can be done for us unless we are positively receptive, but when we realize the law and how it works, then we will provide that complete inner acceptance. By so doing we permit the Spirit to do the work, to make the gift.

September 12th

Eugene Del Mar

In the Science of Numbers the solution of problems is dependent upon one's perception of principles. It is so in the Science of Life. In one's daily experiences the problems of life are involved, and these may be solved only through his perception and comprehension of the principles of life. As the solution of mathematical problems leads to the realization of the truth of the principles involved, so the solution of life's problems leads to the realization of the truths of Being. Experience, perception and realization are representative respectively of the physical, intellectual and spiritual planes of being. One's perception of principle is tested and converted into realization through the avenue of experience. It is through the test of experience that he acquires knowledge of and faith in that which he believes to be true. That which is absorbed by the intellect, thereafter is assimilated by the understanding through the activities of life. The physical, intellectual and spiritual are inseparable, and each is equally essential. In order to assimilate a truth completely one must make it his own on all three planes. This demands physical manifestation, intellectual expression and spiritual realization. Most truths are capable of presentation in a manner acceptable to the average intellect, but intellectual perception alone is insufficient for practical demonstration. Truth must be tested in the laboratory of physical activity. The physical and intellectual faculties are the instrumentalities for the Soul's realization.

September 13th

Robert Collier

You remember the story of the poor Boer farmer who struggled for years to glean a livelihood out of his rocky soil, only to give it up in despair and go off to seek his fortune elsewhere. Years later, coming back to his old farm, he found it swarming with machinery and life — more wealth being dug out of it every day than he had ever dreamed existed. It was the great Kimberley Diamond Mine! Most of us are like that poor Boer farmer. We struggle along under our surface power, never dreaming of the giant power that could be ours if we would but dig a little deeper — rouse that great Inner Self who can give us more even than any acre of diamonds. As Orison Swett Marden put it: — The majority of failures in life are simply the victims of their mental defeats. Their conviction that they cannot succeed as others do robs them of that vigor and determination which self-confidence imparts, and they don't even half try to succeed. There is no philosophy by which a man can do a thing when he thinks he can't. The reason why millions of men are plodding along in mediocrity today, many of them barely making a living, when they have the ability to do something infinitely bigger, is because they lack confidence in themselves. They don't believe they can do the bigger thing that would lift them out of their rut of mediocrity and poverty; they are not winners mentally.

September 14th

Venice J. Bloodworth

Let us assume that you have rid yourself of every idea of lack or limit and have established a consciousness of truth and freedom and are now ready to rebuild yourself physically and financially. You must now realize your relation to your fellow man and the fact that every human being possesses the same indwelling power that you now recognize as your greatest asset. It is good to keep this fact in mind because it will help you to realize that any distressing condition is only a mistake and that it is in your power to help erase all such conditions by holding firmly to the fact that health, wealth, and happiness are omnipresent. Such a realization on your part will keep you from being critical and impatient with the mistakes of your brother. If he does not understand his own power, he is a child moving in darkness and is entitled to your help. Hold all men in mind as being healthy, happy, and prosperous. When you do this you are helping others and sowing good for yourself. Always send out thoughts of love and service. They will come back to you laden with their kind.

September 15th

Ernest Holmes

The sooner we get away from the thought that we have to create, the sooner we will be able to work in line with the Spirit. Always man uses; he never creates anything. The united intelligence of the human race could not make a single rosebud; it does not know enough. But our slightest thought adrift in mind causes the same power that makes all things to create for us. The great error of the race is, and always has been, that men have thought to give a physical reason for things. When that reason has not answered the problems of life they have sought out some other reason just as physical. The fact that they are all wrong is shown in that every generation has found a different reason. When truth is found it will also be found that it never changes to suit the whims of the human fancy. This is proven by the fact that whatever of the real truth the race has discovered has never been changed. The truth that was revealed to the prophets of old has never changed; it is the same today as it was thousands of years ago.

September 16th

Orison Swett Marden

It is nonsense for skeptics and materialists to say that they take no stock in anything that they cannot test with their senses, when we know that the real force in the very things we live on, the elements that nourish and keep alive even the material part of us, are all invisible. We cannot see the life-building, life-sustaining gases in the air we breathe; we cannot see the air, yet we take it into our body eighteen or twenty times a minute and get the silent, unseen power resident in it. The blood absorbs and sends it to the billions of cells in our bodies. None of its mysterious potency can we see or handle, yet we know we could not live a minute without it. No one has ever seen the force in the food we eat, but we know it is there, that we get strength from it, and that after a time the apparently dead, inert matter comes to life in the body; that it acts, dreams, has experiences, works, and creates. Notwithstanding all its marvelous discoveries, science has not been able to uncover the secrets of the unseen forces everywhere at work in the universe. Who can see or explain the mystery of the unfolding bud, the expanding flower, the generating of the wonderful fragrance and marvelous beauty of the rose? Yet we know that there is reality back of them, an intelligence which plans and shapes them, brings them to their glorious maturity. We know that all these things come from the same. Omnipotent Source, that they are the creations of Divine Mind. Scientists are demonstrating that there is but one substance, one eternal force or essence, in the universe, and that all we see is a varying expression of it. To the senses this universal substance, which is the great reality back of all we see, is nonexistent. We can neither see, nor touch, nor taste, nor smell it. Yet all the time science is piling up proof after proof that everything about us is merely a modification, a change of form, change of vibration of this universal substance, just as electricity is a manifestation of force in various forms.

September 17th

James Allen

Habit is repetition. Man repeats the same thoughts, the same actions, the same experiences over and over again until they are incorporated with his being, until they are built into his character as part of himself. Faculty is fixed habit. Evolution is mental accumulation. Man, today, is the result of millions of repetitious thoughts and acts. He is not readymade, he becomes, and is still becoming. His character is predetermined by his own choice. The thought, the act, which he chooses, that, by habit, he becomes.

September 18th

Joseph Murphy

Many liken the subconscious mind to a bank; you are constantly making deposits in this universal bank. Be sure you deposit seeds of peace, harmony, faith, and goodwill; these will be magnified a thousand fold; then prosperity and good fortune will be your harvest. How do you find yourself reacting to the problems of the day and to your environment? If you react with anger, bitterness, criticism, and resentment, you are making these deposits in the bank within you. When you need strength, faith, and confidence, you cannot draw them out, because you have not placed these qualities in your bank. Begin now to deposit joy, love, peace, and good humor; busy your mind with these things; then the subconscious bank will give you compound interest. It will magnify exceedingly beyond your wildest dreams.

September 19th

Ernest Holmes

Begin to blot out, one by one, all false beliefs, all idea that man is limited or poor or miserable. Use that wonderful power of will that God has given to you. Refuse to think of failure or to doubt your own power. See only what you wish to experience, and look at nothing else. No matter how many times the old thought returns, destroy it by knowing that it has no power over you; look it squarely in the face and tell it to go; it does not belong to you, and you must know — and stick to it — that you are now free. Rise up in all the faith of one who knows what he is dealing with, and declare that you are one with Infinite Mind. Know that you cannot get away from this One Mind; that wherever you may go, there, right beside you, waiting to be used, is all the power there is in the whole universe. When you realize this you will know that in union with this, the only power, you are more than all else, you are more than anything that can ever happen to you.

September 20th

Prentice Mulford

Thought being substance or force, you can pile up in your mind volumes of that force for or against you. To think of nothing but difficulties and possible troubles in business, is to set your mind as the magnet to attract only difficulties, first in thought, next in substance. This becomes with many a fixed habit hard to get rid of. You have nothing whatever to do with a difficulty but to set your mind as a magnet in the direction for receiving force, ideas, and plans for overcoming that difficulty. If you have trouble with any person, and are always thinking of his injustice toward you, in the mood of anger or complaint, you are in thought element making over again and again the wrangle or battle. You can use up in growling, scolding, complaining, and grumbling, be it thought out silently, or spoken to others, the same force or thought which would make a plan to get rid of the thing scolded or grumbled at. It is on precisely the same principle as the strength with which the mason builds his wall can be used in tearing it down, or in flinging about bricks at random. If you will give your body all the rest it needs, your mental force will work far and near more powerfully for you. Your plans will be deeper, and, when carried out, more productive of results. If the body is always fagged out, much of the force of that spirit must be used up in keeping its hold on the body, — in other words, keeping it alive. It matters not whether you tire yourself out voluntarily, or are obliged to do so to get a living. The result is the same.

September 21st

Uriel Buchanan

Enter the silence and come face to face with the Infinite Power. There you will find the sanctuary where the divine and human blend. There you will find a refuge from the tumult of the world and will gain strength to go forth with a living power which will drive from you all that is morbid or weak. Then you will realize that you already dwell in eternity, in the real, and that the dazzling dream you have had of the future, in some mystical world beyond the skies, may be realized here and now. Then every sense will become alive to the beauties and realities of the eternal present. Then you will know that every tree and plant and flower, the ocean and the vaulted heaven, as well as every human being, live in the radiance of Divine Love, Truth and Goodness. And when you feel this to be true, there is no limit to the power you may draw to you for the accomplishment of the things desired.

September 22nd

Christian Larson

There are a great many people who are disturbed over the fact that they have inherited certain characteristics or ailments from their parents, but what they have inherited is simply subconscious tendencies in that direction, and those tendencies can be changed absolutely. What we inherit from our parents can be eliminated so completely that no one would ever know it had been there. In like manner, we can improve so decidedly upon the good qualities that we have inherited from our parents that any similarity between parent and child in those respects would disappear completely. The subconscious mind is always ready, willing and competent to make any change for the better in our physical or mental make-up that we may desire, though it does not work in some miraculous manner, nor does it usually produce results instantaneously. In most instances its actions are gradual, but they invariably produce the results intended if the proper training continues. The subconscious mind will respond to the directions of the conscious mind so long as those directions do not interfere with the absolute laws of nature. The subconscious never moves against natural law, but it has the power to so use natural law that improvement along any line can be secured. It will reproduce in mind and body any condition that is thoroughly impressed and deeply felt by the conscious mind. It will bring forth undesirable conditions when directed to produce such conditions, and it will bring forth health, strength, youth and added power when so directed.

September 23rd

Ernest Holmes

If, knowing the infinite power flowing through you, you still remain sick and unhappy, miserable and poor, my friend, it is your own fault. Do not blame God, do not blame man, and do not say it is of the devil. It is your own fault. Every time you say I AM, you are recognizing the eternal infinite presence of omnipotent power within yourself, which is God operating through your thought, and that is why you bring upon yourself the thing you fear, and why you bring to yourself the thing you want.

September 24th

Henry Thomas Hamblin

The world may be divided into two classes of people: (1) those who overcome life, and (2) those who are overcome by life. Those who overcome life's difficulties are those who do so in thought. Those who are overcome by life's difficulties, are those who do not overcome in thought. If the latter have not deliberately made a practice of "dodging" unpleasant thoughts in an unfortunate attempt to follow a form of wrong thinking which they erroneously believed to be right-thinking, they yet are passive; that is, they fail to overcome, in thought, the difficulty that must be overcome, sooner or later, in actual experience. The secret of overcoming is in thought victory. If we continually overcome in our thoughts we develop a steadfast mind. Without a steadfast mind it is impossible to be victorious in life's battle. On the other hand, there is no difficulty, capable of human solution, that cannot be overcome by a steadfast mind. Indeed, if a man's mind is steadfastly directed towards a certain object, not only will he be truly successful, but the most remarkable things may happen or be achieved, beyond anything that might be hoped for or expected.

September 25th

Joseph Murphy

The first thing to realize is that your subconscious mind is always working. It is active night and day, whether you act upon it or not. Your subconscious is the builder of your body, but you cannot consciously perceive or hear that inner silent process. Your business is with your conscious mind and not your subconscious mind. Just keep your conscious mind busy with the expectation of the best, and make sure the thoughts you habitually think are based on whatsoever things are lovely, true, just, and of good report. Begin now to take care of your conscious mind, knowing in your heart and soul that your subconscious mind is always expressing, reproducing, and manifesting according to your habitual thinking. Remember, just as water takes the shape of the pipe it flows through, the life principle in you flows through you according to the nature of your thoughts. Claim that the healing presence in your subconscious is flowing through you as harmony, health, peace, joy, and abundance. Think of it as a living intelligence, a lovely companion on the way. Firmly believe it is continually flowing through you vivifying, inspiring, and prospering you. It will respond exactly this way. It is done unto you as you believe.

September 26th

Eugene Del Mar

The image that will appear on the mental mirror of each person will depend upon the condition of the mirror — the degree of its sensitiveness, the texture of the mentality, or the unfoldment of the spiritual understanding. As each of these is individual and unique, it is evident that no two persons sense the outer world in precisely the same way. Not infrequently the difference is an extreme one. In looking without one is really looking within; and what one will vision outside of himself is dependent upon how he has prepared the inner self. If one's mental mirror is blurred or blemished, his vision of the outer world will take on these characteristics. If one's mental mirror be disturbed by fear or hate, his images of the outer world will seem antagonistic or conflicting. If one's mental mirror be placid or serene, in loving or peaceful quiet, the outer world will have a calming or soothing appearance. Looking within, what does one find there? What is the character of one's prevailing thoughts? Are they constructive or destructive, optimistic or pessimistic? Are they loving or hateful, peaceful or antagonistic? Are they hopeful or despondent, full of faith or of doubt? Whatever they are, they affect the mirror, and to that extent determine the image of the outer world upon which one's vision will be centered. Would one change the outer world, in so far as he is concerned? Would one gaze upon a world of form different from the one that now engages his attention? Would one change the world he lives in — his world — from the unpleasant, uninviting, or uninteresting appearance in which it discloses itself to him? Would one see a world quite different from the one he apparently inhabits? There is nothing the matter with the world in itself. There are no inherent discords or inharmonies. Discords are but harmonies not understood. The trouble is entirely in one's misinterpretation. The discords are within. The harmonizer is within also. After the change has been made within the without will change in appearance. There may be no outward change, for none is necessary. One's mental mirror has acquired a different receptivity. Its surface vibrations have changed in their attractions. Its radio activity has acquired an affinity for different rates of vibration.

September 27th

Ernest Holmes

Our words have the power of life within them; that the word is always with us and never far off. The word is within our own mouth. Every time we speak we are using power. We are one in mind with the whole universe; we are all eternally united in this mind with real power. It is our own fault if we do not use this truth after we see it. We should feel ourselves surrounded by this mind, this great pulsating life, this all-seeing and all-knowing reality. When we do feel this near presence, this great power and life, then all we have to do is to speak forth into it, speak with all the positive conviction of the soul that has found its source, and above all else never fear but that it will be done unto us even as we have believed. What wonderful power, what a newness of life and of power of expression, is waiting for those who really believe.

September 28th

Charles Wesley Kyle

The power by which you govern all of this marvelous machinery through which life is expressed is THOUGHT. "As a man thinketh in his heart so is he." If you desire health, THINK HEALTH; if you desire wealth THINK WEALTH, and if you desire LOVE, THINK LOVE, always THINK LOVE for it fulfills every requirement of the law; it meets every possible demand that may be made upon you, and it clears the way of all obstructions. Concentration is the method by which you will win the desire of your heart; it matters not what your trouble may be, concentrated thought will bring you sure and perfect relief. By the positive exercise of thought are you made just what you are and by its exercise you may become whatsoever you will to be. The object and purpose of going into the Silence is that we may contact the higher vibrations — to come in touch with the Source of Universal Energy and 'Power. Herein lies the secret of becoming, for here we are enabled to catch all that we may be enabled to express of the Divinity of being. Happy is he who has found this never failing oasis in the otherwise comparatively lifeless desert of human experience. When you contact this supreme state you will know it; you will never have a doubt about that experience, for no "flash of lightning, however vivid, could have impressed you so much as will this first experience. When you once have experienced the effect of contacting this powerful voltage, you will no longer be enslaved by the bonds of the psychic mind. From the indolent state of the subjective — the world of idle fancies and dreams, in which the many are content to dwell — you will be carried into a practical, sane and sensible plane of life where the power which you have received will call into activity every energy of your whole nature, and your life of action and genuine worth to yourself and others will begin. "We awake to the consciousness of it, we are aware of it (this indefinable plus) coming forth in our mind; but we feel that we did not make it, that it is discovered to us, that it is whether we will or no.

September 29th

Walter C. Lanyon

As you are reading these lines I, the Spirit of the Consciousness of the Presence, am awaiting recognition. You — yes, you, the poor little discounted one, the one who stood farthest from the pulpit, and received scarce a sign of recognition from the consecrated souls — I have come to you, and I AM the same One who has been standing at the door of your consciousness knocking for ages. "Behold I [the Spirit] stand at the door [of your consciousness] and knock. If any [no distinction is made] man will open up to ME, I will come in and sup with him and he with ME." No matter who you are, neither the grade or the length of your teaching, nor the fears of condemnation. You who read this page, do you hear? Do you see? I AM that which will tear the veil of belief, and you shall see, not a little demonstration of supply that will last you for a week, but the fields white with substance, and you shall know that deep in the secret place of your being is the Key to the Universe.

September 30th

Orison Swett Marden

Whatever we visualize intensely and persistently we create, vitalize into form, build into the life, bring into the actual. In other words, the vital substance from which man fashions circumstances, destiny, is in the unseen world where all potencies and power dwell. The very foundations of the universe and the things which are doing most for the world today are the unseen forces, eternal principles. The forces which transport us over the globe and bring its uttermost parts into instant communion; the power of the principles of chemistry, of gravitation, of cohesion, of adhesion, — all the mighty agencies operating in the universe and producing its phenomena, — we cannot see, hear, or touch, we cannot appreciate them with our senses only as we feel their effects;

The Within Creates The Without: Daily Meditations

they are things we know little about, yet we know they are great realities. Who knows or who has seen what is back of these great principles, these potencies which we know exist? Gravitation, which is holding the heavenly bodies in their orbits, which keeps the world so marvelously balanced in space, revolving at terrific speed around the sun, none of them varying in their revolutions in their orbits the fraction of a second in a thousand years, is an invisible force. Because we can't see or taste, or smell, or handle it, shall we say it is not a reality? That it does not exist? We can see and feel the effects of electricity, but who knows what this invisible force is? The Edisons, the Bells, the Marconis have, through experiments, found out certain things, certain laws governing it, through the operation of which we get heat, energy, and light. They have put it to work for us in a multitude of ways. It carries our messages under oceans and across continents. It has already done away with a large part of the drudgery of the world, and is destined to serve mankind in ways perhaps not yet dreamed of by even the wisest scientists and inventors. This mighty force which he has used in his thousands of inventions, Edison confesses he knows nothing about. He stands in awe of this mysterious power which has come out of the cosmic intelligence in response to his efforts. He regards himself merely as a channel through which some of its secrets have been passed along to man, to make life less toilsome, more comfortable, and more beautiful.

October

October 1st

Ernest Holmes

Another thing that we must eliminate is talking about limitation; we must not even think of it or read about it, or have any connection with it in any of our thinking, for we get only that which we think, no more and no less. This will be a hard thing to do. But if we remember that we are working out the science of being, though it may seem long and hard at times we sooner or later do it, and once done it is done forever. Every step in advance is an Eternal step, and will never have to be taken again. We are not building for a day or a year, but we are building for all time and for Eternity. So we will build the more stately mansion under the Supreme wisdom and the unfailing guidance of the Spirit, and we will do unto all, even as we would have them do unto us; there is no other way. The wise will listen, look and learn, then follow what they know to be the only way that is in line with the Divine will and purposes.

October 2nd

Joseph Murphy

All of us should seek an inner guidance for our problems. If you have a financial problem, repeat this before you retire at night: "Now I shall sleep in peace. I have turned this matter over to the God-Wisdom within. It knows only the answer. As the sun rises in the morning, so will my answer be resurrected. I know the sunrise never fails." Then go off to sleep. Do not fret, fuss and fume over a problem. Night brings counsel. Sleep on it. Your intellect cannot solve all your problems. Pray for the Light that is to come. Remember that the dawn always comes; then the shadows flee away. Let your sleep every night be a contented bliss.

October 3rd

Venice J. Bloodworth

The subconscious mind does not think, reason, balance, judge, or reject. It simply accepts all suggestions furnished by the conscious mind whether they be good or evil, constructive or destructive. Herein lies the mighty power of the conscious mind. The subconscious mind receives any idea or belief as a pattern to work by and proceeds to bring such ideas and beliefs into manifestation. Prior to the development of our conscious reasoning power the subconscious mind works by a hereditary pattern, or race instinct. During childhood these subconscious activities are the result of heredity and environment demands and continue to be such unless we are fortunate enough to learn the unlimited power of our subconscious mind, though some people unconsciously draw on this power with most splendid results. Thus we find the secret of good or bad results in child training is due to the fact that whatever training children get leaves its impression on the subconscious mind and makes the habits formed in our tender years the basis for all future actions unless we consciously and systematically set about to change them.

October 4th

Robert Collier

Universal Mind plays no favorites. No one human being has any more power than any other. It is simply that few of us use the power that is in our hands. The great men of the world are in no wise SUPER Beings. They are ordinary creatures like you and me, who have stumbled upon the way of drawing upon their subconscious mind — and through it upon the Universal Mind. Speaking of Henry Ford's phenomenal success, his friend Thomas A. Edison said of him — "He draws upon his subconscious mind." The secret of being what you have it in you to be is simply this: Decide now what it is you want of life, exactly what you wish your future to be. Plan it out in detail. Vision it from start to finish. See yourself as you are now, Being those things you have always wanted to do. Make them REAL in your mind's eye — feel them, live them, believe them, especially at the moment of going to sleep, when it is easiest to reach your subconscious mind — and you will soon be seeing them in real life. It matters not whether you are young or old, rich or poor. The time to begin is NOW. It is never too late.

October 5th

Ernest Holmes

Since all is mind, and it is done unto us as we mentally think, all life is simply a law of thought-activity of consciousness. In our life the power flows through us. If we provide a big receptivity, it will do a big thing; if, on the other hand, we only believe in a small way, the activity must be a small one. The Spirit can do for us only what it can do through us. Unless we are able to provide the consciousness, it cannot make the gift. Few people have a great consciousness, and this explains why so few excel. The power behind all things of itself is without limit; it is all-power; in us it has to become what we make it. We carry within our own soul the key to all expression, but few enter in. The door is not seen with the physical eye, and as yet but few have gained the ability to see; the majority merely look. Realizing, then, that while the power is limitless it must become operative through our own thought, we shall see that what we need is not some greater power, but that what we really need is a greater consciousness, a deeper realization of life, a grander concept of being. We must unify ourselves with the great whole. The man who dares to fling his thought out into universal intelligence with the positive assurance of one who knows and dares to claim all there is will find that it will be done. God will honor his request. On the other hand, the one who fears to speak lest God will smite will find himself smitten of the law, not because God is angry, but because it is done as he believes.

October 6th

Christian Larson

We frequently hear the expression, "I can never do anything right," and it is quite simple to understand that such a mode of thought would train the mind to act below its true ability and capacity. If you are fully convinced that you can never do anything right, it will become practically impossible for you to do anything right at any time, but on the other hand, if you continue to think, "I am going to do everything better and better," it is quite natural that your entire mental system should be inspired and trained to do things better and better. Hundreds of similar expressions could be mentioned, but we are all familiar with them, and from the comments made above, anyone will realize that such expressions are obstacles in our way, no matter what we may do. In right thinking the purpose should be never to use any expression that conveys to your mind what you do not want, or what is detrimental or unwholesome in any manner whatever. Think only what you wish to produce or realize. If trouble is brewing, think about the greater success that you have in mind. If anything adverse is about to take place, do not think of what that adversity may bring, but think of the greater good that you are determined to realize in your life. When trouble is brewing, the average person usually thinks of nothing else. Their mind is filled with fear, and not a single faculty in their possession can do justice to itself. And as trouble is usually brewing in most places, more or less, people have what may be called a chronic expectation for trouble; and as they usually get more or less of what they expect, they imagine they are fully justified in entertaining such expectations. But here it is absolutely necessary to change the mind completely. Whatever our present circumstances may be, we should refuse absolutely to expect anything but the best that we can think of. The whole mind, with all its powers and faculties, should be thrown, so to speak, into line with the optimistic tendency, and whatever comes or not, we should think only of the greater things that we expect to realize. In brief, we should concentrate the mind absolutely upon whatever goal we may have in view, and I should look neither to the left nor to the right.

The Within Creates The Without: Daily Meditations

October 7th

James Allen

No man is helplessly bound. The very law by which he has become a self-bound slave, will enable him to become a self-emancipated master. To know this, he has but to act upon it — that is, to deliberately and strenuously abandon the old lines of thought and conduct, and diligently fashion new and better lines. That he may not accomplish this in a day, a week, a month, a year, or five years, should not dishearten and dismay him. Time is required for the new repetitions to become established, and the old ones to be broken up; but the law of habit is certain and infallible, and a line of effort patiently pursued and never abandoned, is sure to be crowned with success; for if a bad condition, a mere negation, can become fixed and firm, how much more surely can a good condition, a positive principle, become established and powerful!

October 8th

Uriel Buchanan

The measure of man's success in any direction is determined by the predominant state of his mind. If you are hopeful, enthusiastic and courageous, and do not yield to the influence of despondency and doubt, you are sending out forces which will attract the good; and as your faith becomes stronger in your ability to control and direct your thoughts, you will absorb the finer elements which bring health, peace, happiness and all things desired. It is difficult to keep permanently in a hopeful, confident mood of mind, as there are times when progress is slow and the opposing influences seem greater than the forces which aid. But the man who has faith in his power, the man who sees only the good and knows that from every experience will come more strength and greater persistency, wisdom and courage, will bend all things to his purpose and make every circumstance aid him in material advancement. Having a definite aim always in view, a thought force is generated which is felt by all with whom you have dealings.

October 9th

Ernest Holmes

To acquire the larger consciousness is no easy task. All that we have believed in which contradicts the perfect whole must be dropped from our thought, and we must come to realize that we are now living in a perfect universe, peopled with perfect spiritual beings, each of which (coupled with the Great Divinity) is complete within himself. We must see that we are one in the great one, and then we will not separate or divide, but unite and add to, until in time we will find that we are living in an entirely different world from that in which we had once thought we were living. Of course this will meet with much opposition from those unenlightened souls whom we must contact in the world. But what of that? Remember, the great man is the one who can keep in the crowd the calm, even thought, the deep, divine reliance on principle. And more, this is the only way to help or to save the world. In time all people will come to the same understanding. You are lifting up the standard of life, and those who are ready will follow. You have no responsibility to save the world except by exemplifying the truth. The world must save itself.

October 10th

Prentice Mulford

Our thoughts, or in other words, our state of mind, is ever at work "fixing up "things good or bad for us in advance. As you cultivate this state of mind more and more you will at last have no need of reminding yourself to get into such mood. Because the mood will have become a part of your everyday nature, and you cannot then get out of it, or prevent the pleasant experiences it will bring you. Our real self is that which we cannot see, hear, or feel with the physical senses — our mind. The body is an instrument it uses. We are then made up entirely of forces we call thoughts. When these thoughts are evil or immature they bring us pain and ill-fortune. We can always change them for better thoughts or forces. Earnest steady desire for a new mind (or self) will surely bring the new mind and more successful self. And this will ever be changing through such desire for the newer and ever more successful self.

October 11th

Venice J. Bloodworth

We sow our thoughts in our subconscious mind and the law of growth brings them into visible expression. If our thoughts are positive in faith, desire, courage, determination, cheerfulness and love, our physical condition and environment will express these qualities in health, happiness and prosperity. But if our thoughts are fear, hatred, envy, anxiety, grief or jealousy, we will reap these results in poverty, disease and misery. Every time you think, you start a chain of causation that will create a condition in strict accord with the quality of thought which originated it. Whether we have success or failure, it comes by the operation of exactly the same principle; the principle is unchangeable; its operation is exact; we use the same principle and the same substance to bring either good or bad results. It is the seed you sow that determines the nature of your product.

October 12th

Eugene Del Mar

If one's reaping is of his own sowing it is not of others' sowing. He cannot consistently accept the former conception, and at the same time blame others for his reaping. When he praises himself for his pleasurable sensations and experiences, and blames others for the painful ones, his inconsistency is the outcome of a dualistic conception. The operation of One Principle equally attracts both what one interprets as agreeable and as disagreeable. It is his interpretation that determines his relation to experiences and environments. One determines his own fate. All one's experiences and environments are the result of his own comparative ignorance or wisdom. If he reap what he sow, there is no sufficient reason for complaining of others, or of harboring ill-will or unkind feeling. Inherently either one is or is a mental state) will have harsh, unlovely features. One with a gentle disposition will have a smiling and serene countenance. All the other organs of the human body are equally responsive to thought. Who has not seen the face become red with rage or white with fear? Who has not known of people who became desperately ill following an outburst of temper? Physicians declare that just as fear, irritability and hate distort the features, they likewise distort the heart, stomach and liver.

October 16th

Henry Thomas Hamblin

There are two old proverbs which are well known and often quoted, but whose profound psychological importance is not perhaps fully appreciated. They are these: "Birds of a feather flock together," and "You can tell a man's character by the company he keeps." The source of this attraction is largely in a man's thought. If we think thoughts of a certain type, then we attract to ourselves people of a similar type of thought. We are drawn together by the invisible forces of attraction. It is true that the character of our thoughts becomes, in course of time, written on our face, so that all the world can see if we are pure or filthy, strong or weak, loving or hard, noble or base; but it is largely the attractive power of thought that draws people to us. Our thoughts not only attract people to us after their kind, but they also attract other thoughts after their kind, and also opportunities and circumstances. The human mind, although in one sense it can be called creative, is more of a receptacle of thought than a generator of the same. We have as it were, two doors to our mind, one opening to a stream of heavenly, good, beautiful, ennobling, healthful and wholesome thoughts; the other opening to a stream of undesirable, weakening, destructive thoughts. It is impossible to have both of these doors open at the same time. When we think thoughts of purity, wholeness, charity, etc. — in other words, thoughts of a Heavenly character — then the door to Heaven and all that is beautiful is opened, allowing a flood of similar thoughts to enter. This is why prayer is so valuable. Prayer is the raising of the thought and attention, also the heart and affections, to Heaven. In response there is a return flow or influx of Divine life, thought and ideas. One who perseveres in this practice becomes, in course of time, so changed by this Divine influx as to be heavenly minded. Then the other door leading to all that is undesirable remains shut always.

October 17th

Ernest Holmes

Dare to say, "Behold I AM he. Great men have come and gone, and behold a greater now stands here where I stand, and I AM that one." The world will laugh and perhaps scorn. The Christian world will hold up its hands in holy horror, lest you blaspheme; the unchristian world will smile knowingly. Neither the one nor the other will understand, but the understanding of either counts for nothing. You are now free, and your freedom will yet save the world from itself. The great soul finds within himself the Divine companionship which he needs. He finds within himself the "Peace which passeth all understanding" and the power to do all things. All Power! He speaks, his word is Law and it is done unto him of all the power there is. His word knows itself to be the law of life unto all for whom it is spoken and who receive it.

October 18th

Orison Swett Marden

I know of no one thing that will have a greater influence upon your life than the forming of the habit of thinking of yourself as lucky, regarding yourself as extremely fortunate in your birth, in your location, in your adaptation to your particular line of work, as fortunate in your ambition and in your chance in life to make good. We are just beginning to learn that we are made, fashioned and molded by our thoughts, which are forces as real as is the force of electricity. Our thought is constantly shaping us to correspond with it. We are our own architects, our own sculptors. We are always reshaping, remolding ourselves to fit our thoughts and our emotions, our motives, our general attitude towards life. If we think of ourselves as being always lucky, we may not be extraordinary examples of good luck, but we shall always be happy, smiling and contented, believing that everything that comes to us is the best that we could possibly attain.

October 19th

James Allen

Dwelling upon one's petty troubles and ailments is a manifestation of weakness of character. To so dwell upon them in thought leads to frequent talking about them, and this, in turn, impresses them more vividly upon the mind, which soon becomes demoralized by such petting and pitying. It is as convenient to dwell upon happiness and health as upon misery and disease; as easy to talk about them, and much more pleasant and profitable to do so.

October 20th

Charles Wesley Kyle

No thing wants you unless you first want it. You attract what you are. If you want anything you must, in essence, become that thing, when the supreme law of attraction, of growth, will be put in operation against which there is no power that can keep you from the thing you may desire. You are a supreme magnet in the great field of cosmic energy, charged with the power to draw your own to yourself. The result of the highest revelation, using that word in the plain sense and meaning that whenever any fact that was unknown to us is made known, that it is revealed, shows that there is but one substance; that mind is universal, and, consequently in everything; that thought is the creator, and that all that is, is the product of thought. All things spring from one source, and that source being infinite, it follows that no thing ever was or ever can be separated from it; space when used in this connection being an illusion. Everything, percept, concept, thought, form and act is included in the infinite. Infinity can have no thing opposed to it. We only oppose ourselves from a lack of the knowledge of Unity. The expression of Jesus, "I and my Father are one," clearly sets out his understanding of the truth of Unity. Harmony, peace and perfection are meaningless words unless founded upon the presupposition of Unity, and a lack of the understanding of this law and its application, has been the cause of all the trouble in the world. A comprehension of this law constitutes the supreme lesson for man to learn.

October 21st

Ernest Holmes

The best way to arrive at the highest consciousness is to have a great faith in the willingness and the ability of Life to do all for us, by working through us. We must believe in the inherent goodness and all-powerfulness of the Spirit of Truth. And so every path leads us back to the one point and we must learn to realize the near presence, the great reality. There, through the door of our own thought, we enter into the Universal Consciousness, into a complete realization of life and truth, of love and beauty; and as we sit in the silence of our own souls and listen, it will be the greatest thing that we will ever do. In that completeness we are lost and yet we are found. This is what is meant that a man must lose his life in order to find it. We are lost to the human and found in the divine. We realize that we are One with Cause.

October 22nd

Christian Larson

If we try to train the subconscious to produce a certain amount, it might be some time before that amount can be developed. In the meantime, we should meet disappointment and delay, but if our desire is for steady increase along all lines from where we stand now, we shall be able to secure, first, a slight improvement and then added improvement to be followed with still greater improvement until we finally reach the highest goal we have in view. No effort should be made to destroy those qualities that we may not desire. Whatever we think about deeply or intensely, the subconscious will take up and develop further. Therefore, if we think about our failings, shortcomings or bad habits, the continually rejected the very fundamental of justice, wisdom, and love. In its essence, the truth of the Golden Rule should be evident to every rational mind. It is no more than a special setting of the fundamental principle of action and reaction, from the operation of which there is no possible escape. As this basic truth is essentially beneficent in its operation, so likewise is the Golden Rule. The reason it has not found universal acceptance is simply because personal selfishness and egotism have blinded man to even the simplest truths. That honesty is the best policy, that it were well to do unto others that which one would have others do unto him, likewise to love one's neighbor as one's self, each and all are injunctions to comply with the fundamental principle of action and reaction. Not only this, but any falling away from these conceptions is a departure from principle, and the occasion for discord, inharmony, and disease. As long as the truth remains impractical, it is falsehood alone that will be looked upon as practical; and the reactions of falsehood are found in the individual and social conditions in which humanity is now immersed.

October 29th

Ernest Holmes

Limitation is an experience of the race, but it is not the fault of God, it is the fault of man's perception. And to prove that this is so, let any man break the bonds of this false sense of life and he at once begins to express less and less limitation. It is a matter of the growth of the inner idea. People often say when they are told this, "Do you think that I decided to be poor and miserable; do you take me for a fool?" No, you are not a fool, but it is quite possible that you have been fooled, and most of us have been. I know of no one who has escaped being fooled about life; you may not have had thoughts of poverty but at the same time you may have had thoughts that have produced it. Just watch the process of your thinking and see how many times a day you think something that you would not want to happen. This will satisfy you that you need to be watchful, that your thought needs to be controlled. What we need to do is to reverse the process of our thinking and see to it that we think only positive, constructive thoughts. A calm determination to think just what we want to think regardless of conditions will do much to put us on the highway to a greater realization of life.

October 30th

Shirley Bell Hastings

Take the Lord's Prayer, write it down, study it. Then think over this translation:

"Our Force that is within us, holy and sacred is Thy nature.
Come forth and do for us on the outer as we are thinking.
Give to us now all that we need for this demonstration.
Give for our ignorance thy bright wisdom.
As we give for the lack we find in others.
Let us not be led into the temptation of wrongly using You.
Deliver us from imperfection.
Thine is the power and to Thee be the thanks forever.
Amen."

Withdraw into the closet of mind; close out the outer; speak to the Force, the Father, the Source, the Principle, the Cause of all things. "As I give, so do I receive" is a universal law.

October 31st

James Allen

The thoughtless, the ignorant, and the indolent, seeing only the apparent effects of things and not the things themselves, talk of luck, of fortune, and chance. See a man grow rich, they say, "How lucky he is!" Observing another become intellectual, they exclaim, "How highly favored he is!" And noting the saintly character and wide influence of another, the remark, "How chance aids him at every turn!" They do not see the trials and failures and struggles which these men have voluntarily encountered in order to gain their experience. They have no knowledge of the sacrifices they have made, of the undaunted efforts they have put forth, of the faith they have exercised, that they might overcome the apparently insurmountable, and realize the Vision of their heart. They do not know the darkness and the heartaches; they only see the light and joy, and call it "luck"; do not see the long and arduous journey, but only behold the pleasant goal, and call it "good fortune"; do not understand the process, but only perceive the result, and call it "chance."

November

The Within Creates The Without: Daily Meditations

November 1st

Christian Larson

Thought is the one original cause of the conditions, characteristics and peculiarities of the human personality, and everything that appears in the personality is the direct or indirect effect of the various actions of thought. It is therefore evident that man naturally grows into the likeness of the thought he thinks, and it is also evident that the nature of his thought would be determined by that which he thinks of the most. The understanding of this fact will reveal to all minds the basic law of change, and though it is basic, its intelligent use may become simplicity itself. Through the indiscriminate use of this law, man has constantly been changing, sometimes for the better, sometimes not, but by the conscious, intelligent, use of this law he may change only for the better and as rapidly as the sum total of his present ability will permit. The fact that mental conditions and dispositions may be changed through the power of thought, will readily be accepted by every mind, but that mental qualities, abilities, personal appearances and physical conditions may be changed in the same way all minds may not be ready to accept. Nevertheless, that thought can change anything in the human system, even to a remarkable degree, is now a demonstrated fact. We have all seen faces change for the worse under the influence of grief, worry and misfortune, and we have observed that all people grow old who expect to do so, regardless of the fact that the body of the octogenarian is not a day older than the body of a little child. We have unlimited evidence to prove that ability will improve or deteriorate according to the use that is made of the mind. A man's face reveals his thought, and we can invariably detect the predominating states of the mind that lives in a groove. When a person changes their mental states at frequent intervals, no one state has the opportunity to produce an individual, clear-cut expression, and therefore cannot be so readily detected, but where one predominating state is continued in action for weeks or months or years, anyone can say what that state is, by looking at the face of the one who has it. Thus we can detect different kinds of disposition, different grades of mind, different degrees of character and different modes of living, and convince ourselves at the same time, that man in general, looks, acts and lives the way he thinks.

November 2nd

Ernest Holmes

There is no special creation for any individual, but we all specialize the law every time we think into it. For all our thought is taken up and something is always done with it. A good practice is to sit and realize that you are a center of Divine attraction, that all things are coming to you, that the power within is going out and drawing back all that you will ever need. Don't argue about it, just do it, and when you have finished leave it all to the Law, knowing that it will be done. Declare that all life, all love and power are now in your life. Declare that you are now in the midst of plenty. Stick to it even though you may not as yet see the result. It will work and those who believe the most always get the most. Think of the Law as your friend. always looking out for your interest. Trust completely in it and it will bring your good to you.

November 3rd

Mrs. Evelyn Lowes Wicker

Mental Impressions. This subtle force, when in the ether, is neutral. It has not a mental impression. Energy is negative. Mind is positive. The negative force — energy — is waiting to be played upon by the positive force — mind. When we appropriate through the breathing apparatus this energy from the atmosphere it becomes ours. As soon as assimilated it at once takes on the predominant mental impression of the subconscious mind. The predominant mental impression always impresses energy as soon as that energy becomes a part of us. If the predominant thought of the subconscious mind is failure, energy becomes laden with the thought of failure, and from the moment that energy is so impressed success to you is an impossible thing. When energy becomes impressed with the thought of illness there is no hope of you becoming well until you change your predominant mental impression into one of health. It is hard to do, but it is absolutely necessary. You have to talk to yourself; you have to talk to your great subconscious mind and declare, and affirm until you have dominated the situation — until all the energy that you possess is charged with thoughts of health. The predominant mental impression governs the expression of energy.

November 4th

Robert Collier

You are only as old as your mind. Every function, every activity of your body, is controlled by your mind. Your vital organs, your blood that sends the material for rebuilding to every cell and tissue, the processes of elimination that remove all the broken down and waste material, all are dependent for their functioning upon the energy derived from your mind. The human body can be compared to an electric transportation system. When the dynamo runs at full power every car speeds along, and everything is handled with precision. But let the dynamo slow down and the whole system lags. That dynamo is your mind, and your thoughts provide the energy that runs it. Feed it thoughts of health and vigor and your whole system will reflect energy and vitality. Feed it thoughts of decrepitude and age, and you will find it slowing down to the halting pace you set for it. You can grow old at 30. You can be young at 90. It is up to you. Which do you choose? If you choose youth, then start this minute renewing your youth. Find a picture — or, better still, a statuette — of the man you would like to be, the form you would like to have. Keep it in your room. When you go to bed at night, visualize it in your mind's eye — hold it in your thought as YOU — as the man YOU ARE GOING TO BE!

November 5th

Venice J. Bloodworth

Of course, you did not consciously ask for poor health or financial embarrassment or anything else that you do not want, but not knowing the importance of controlling your thoughts, you went along with no definite end in view, no goal, blown along by Dick, Tom, and Harry's opinions; letting your mind sop up any opinion or statement without asking yourself whether such opinions were based on real facts or not, until you find yourself with a lot of beliefs, impressions, and opinions that have no foundation whatsoever. Now, if the Law works to bring about undesirable conditions on the hit or miss plan that most people use, it will certainly work better to produce conditions that are systematically thought out and concentrated upon with a definite end in view. In fact, it will work much better to bring good conditions, because good is in accord with principle, and every time the beautiful, joyous possibilities of realizing your ambitions seem too good to be true just get the fact that mind or thought is the ONLY CREATOR; that thinking is real, the true business of life; and that your results will be in exact accord, both in kind and quality, with your thoughts.

November 6th

Ernest Holmes

Here are a few simple rules for prosperity that are as sure of working as that water is sure to be wet. First remember that nothing happens by chance. All is law and all is order. You create your own laws every time you think. There is something, call it what you will, but there is a Power around you that knows and that understands all things. This Power works like the soil; it receives the seed of your thought and at once begins to operate upon it. It will receive whatever you give to it and will create for you and throw back at you whatever you think into it.

November 7th

Uriel Buchanan

There are three realms of mind: the subconscious, the conscious and the super conscious. The conscious mind belongs purely to the objective world, using the five senses as instruments. The subconscious mind is the stored up memories acquired by the conscious mind during the past years of its search for knowledge and experience on the human plane. The super conscious mind has the power of recognition of thought by a sympathetic process, without the use of the five material channels of sensation. So many instances of unusual power in this direction have come to the notice of scientific investigators that the world has been convinced of this phenomenal keenness of mind. It has been demonstrated beyond question that there is a faculty of perception in the mind which can know what is taking place about it by means independent of the five senses. The super conscious mind, or subliminal self, is as real as the human form, yet it has no weight or measure, and is unlike anything we can see, or touch or analyze. The microscope does not reveal it. Deepest thought and purest reason fail to discover its origin, its nature and destiny. Yet it is within the mind of man, substantial and luminous. The body changes, thoughts come and go, our relations to the great world at large are altered, hopes and loves are born in the heart, live, desire and perish, and others come and go in their place in endless succession; yet through all the shifting scenes in the visible world, there is something within which remains steadfast and true, shedding its mysterious luster through the enchanted realms of mind. By the medium of the super conscious mind you are brought into conscious relationship with the Infinite Power, from which you can draw the energy needed to supply all the demands of your nature.

November 8th

Christian Larson

When you begin to make a positive determined use of those powers in yourself that are already in Positive action, you draw forth into action powers within you that have been dormant, and as this process continues, you will find that you will accumulate volume, capacity and power in your mental world, until you finally become a mental giant. As you begin to grow and become more capable, you will find that you will meet better and better opportunities, not only opportunities for promoting external success, but opportunities for further building yourself up along the lines of ability, capacity and talent. You thus demonstrate the law that "Nothing succeeds like success," and "To him that hath shall be given." And here it is well to remember that it is not necessary to possess external things in the beginning to be counted among them "that hath.." It is only necessary in the beginning to possess the interior riches; that is, to take control of what is in you, and proceed to use it positively with a definite goal in view. He who has control of his own mind has already great riches. He has sufficient wealth to be placed among those who have. He is already successful, and if he continues as he has begun, his success will soon appear in the external world. Thus the wealth that existed at first in the internal only will take shape and form in the external. This is a law that is unfailing, and there is not a man or woman on the face of the earth that cannot apply it with the most satisfying results.

November 9th

Charles Fillmore

The realm of causes may be compared to steam in a glass boiler. If the glass is clear one may look right at it and see nothing at all. Yet when an escape valve is touched the steam rushes out, condenses and becomes visible. But in this process it has also lost its power. Substance exists in a realm of ideas and is powerful when handled by one who is familiar with its characteristics. The ignorant open the valves of the mind and let ideas flow out into a realm with which they have nothing in common. The powerful ideas of substance are condensed into thoughts of time and space, which ignorance conceives as being necessary to their fruition. Thus their power is lost, and a weary round of seedtime and harvest is inaugurated to fulfill the demands of the world. It is the mind that believes in personal possessions that limits the full idea. God's world is a world of results that sequentially follow demands. It is in this kingdom that man finds his true home. Labor has ceased for him who has found this inner kingdom. Divine supply is brought forth without laborious struggle: to desire is to have fulfillment.

November 10th

Ernest Holmes

The one who wishes to practice metaphysics must first, last, and all the time realize that he himself is a center of the divine activity; he must know that whatever God is in the Universal, he is in the world in which he lives. He must know that all things are made out of Spirit, which is First Cause; nothing comes before Spirit. Operating upon itself out of itself, it makes what it will out of its own perfect desire. He must think of the Spirit as the Father of his own life, eternally bound to him, eternally binding him to it.

November 11th

Genevieve Behrend

"As a man thinketh in his heart, so is he" is the law of life, and the Creative Power can no more change this law than an ordinary mirror can reflect back to you a different image than the object you hold before it. "As you think, so are you" does not mean "as you tell people you think," or "as you would wish the world to believe you think." It means your innermost thoughts; that place where no one but you know. "None can know the Father save the son," and "No one can know the son but the Father." Only the reproductive Creative Spirit of Life knows what you think until your thoughts become physical facts and manifest themselves in your body, your brain, or your affairs. Then everyone with whom you come into contact may know, because the Father, the Intelligent Creative Energy which heareth in secret your most secret thoughts, rewards you openly reproduces your thoughts in physical form. "As you think, that is what you become" should be kept in the background of your mind constantly. This is watching and praying without ceasing, and when you are not feeling quite up to par physically, pray.

November 12th

Joseph Murphy

Being a former chemist, I would like to point out that if you combine hydrogen and oxygen in the proportions of two atoms of the former to one of the latter, water would be the result. You are very familiar with the fact that one atom of oxygen and one atom of carbon will produce carbon monoxide, a poisonous gas. But, if you add another atom of oxygen, you will get carbon dioxide, a harmless gas, and so on throughout the vast realm of chemical compounds. You must not think that the principles of chemistry, physics, and mathematics differ from the principles of your subconscious mind. Let us consider a generally accepted principle: "Water seeks its own level." This is a universal principle, which is applicable to water everywhere. Consider another principle: "Matter expands when heated." This is true anywhere, at any time, and under all circumstances. You can heat a piece of steel, and it will expand regardless whether the steel is found in China, England, or India. It is a universal truth that matter expands when heated. It is also a universal truth that whatever you impress on your subconscious mind is expressed on the screen of space as condition, experience, and event.

November 13th

R. C. Douglass

How does one's thought affect his health? How does his word become his "burden"? Through the mind's imaging faculty, for the mind is a delicately constructed camera in which all our thoughts are pictured before they appear in outward expression, in bodily conditions. Eziekel, the greatest of seers, shows us that camera in the following words, "Son of man, hast thou seen what the Elders of Israel do in the dark, every man in his chamber of imagery?" This mental camera is the "dark chamber of imagery," where all our thoughts are pictured before they are brought into expression in painful conditions. We should use this great and important faculty to picture on the sensitive plate of consciousness in the mind's camera things beautiful and true, lovely and harmonious, if we wish the bodily expression beautiful, symmetrical, healthy and harmonious. By the misuse of this faculty we may debase, make sick, or even destroy our bodies; or by the correct use we may purify and rejuvenate them, according to the character of the pictures we make in our mental camera.

November 14th

Ernest Holmes

Everything that we see is the result of mind in action. We all have a body and we have what is called a physical environment; we could have neither if it were not for mind. The law implanted within us is, that we need nothing except ourselves and this All-Wise Creative Mind to make anything; and that just so far as we depend upon any condition, past, present or future, or upon any individual, we are creating chaos, because we are dealing with conditions and not with causes. Every living soul is a law unto himself, but of this great truth few people are conscious. It seems difficult for the race, which feels itself to be so limited, to comprehend the fact that there is a power that makes things directly out of itself, by simply becoming the thing that it makes, and that it does this by self knowing. But we will not demonstrate until we see at least some of this, the greatest truth about life.

November 15th

Robert Collier

Suppose there's a position you want the general manager-ship of your Company. See yourself — just as you are now — sitting in the general manager's chair. See your name on his door. See yourself handling his affairs as you would handle them. Get that picture impressed upon your subconscious mind. See it! Believe it! The Genie-of-your-Mind will find the way to make it come true. The keynote of successful visualization is this: See things as you would have them be instead of as they are. Close your eyes and make clear mental pictures. Make them look and act just as they would in real life. In short, day dream — but day dream with a purpose. Concentrate on the one idea to the exclusion of all others, and continue to concentrate on that one idea until it has been accomplished. Do you want an automobile? A home? A factory? They can all be won in the same way. They are in their essence all of them ideas of mind, and if you will but build them up in your own mind first, stone by stone, complete in every detail, you will find that the Genie-of-your-Mind can build them up similarly in the material world.

November 16th

Shirley Bell Hastings

The Force creates for you as you think. The more trust you have in the power of the Force to take you out of your past trend of thinking and take you toward the fulfillment of the new idea, the faster you go that way. But, whether you have faith or not, the law is there — "As a man thinketh in his heart, so is he." Let us wake up to this law. Let us think of things as we want them to be, not as they are. Resolve now to do your own thinking. Be the divine thinker of your own thoughts. No one else must do your thinking for you. No one else must splash his ideas all over you, all over your mind, for you to work out. If someone is making you unhappy, start a different trend (your own trend) of thinking. Go within your chamber of mind as frequently as necessary and know that no one has the power to make you unhappy unless you accept the idea and permit it to take root in you. "No weapon that is formed against thee shall prosper; and every tongue that shall rise against thee in judgment thou shalt condemn. This is the heritage of the servants of the Lord, and their righteousness is of me, saith the Lord." (Isa. 54:17.) Think happiness and happiness will come to you. You are the way to your own happiness. You can think the happy idea and soon you will find happiness about you. The Force is the Great Servant. It works out the ideas we give to it.

November 17th

James Allen

Each man is as low or high, as little or great, as base or noble as his thoughts; no more, no less. Each moves within the sphere of his own thoughts, and that sphere is his world. In that world in which he forms his habits of thought, he finds his company. He dwells in the region which harmonizes with his particular growth. But he need not perforce remain in the lower worlds. He can lift his thoughts and ascend. He can pass above and beyond into higher realms, into happier habitations. When he chooses and wills he can break the carapace of selfish thought, and breathe the purer airs of a more expansive life.

November 18th

Ernest Holmes

We should realize that we are dealing with the principle that is scientifically correct. It will never fail us at any time but is eternally present. We can approach the Infinite Mind with a depth of thought and understanding, knowing that it will respond, knowing that we are dealing with reality. Jesus, who saw this very clearly, laid down the whole law of life in a few simple words: "It is done unto you as you believe." We do not have to do it, it is done unto us, it is done by a power that is all. Could we believe that a material mountain would be moved, it would be done unto us. But unless we do believe there is no impulse for the creative power and we do not receive. Life externalizes at the level of our thought.

November 19th

Venice J. Bloodworth

The conscious mind must reach understanding through the vibratory action of thought, and it is necessary for us to study with undivided attention anything we desire to learn. Your thought forces will lead you to the realization of your fondest dreams, but make no mistake in thinking these lessons are the royal road to so-called miracles. Psychology is the royal road to undreamed happiness, freedom and success, but you must pay the price of concentration and study or this "Golden Key" is not for you. All possession is based on consciousness and you must establish a consciousness through understanding. A transfer of material things can be made, but wisdom must be bought by our own efforts.

November 20th

Christian Larson

If you are receiving all that you deserve, make yourself more deserving, and you will receive more; but if you are not receiving your share, learn the reason why. If you are to blame, change yourself; if your present work is to blame, use your present work as a steppingstone to something better. The average person, who thinks he is underpaid, will find himself to be the real cause; therefore, the change of himself is the remedy. And he is usually to blame in this respect, that he overvalues his work and undervalues himself. No one can advance in life unless he values himself correctly. The man who lives a "common" life, and continues in "ordinary" attitudes of mind will stay "down," no matter how hard he works or how well he performs his particular labor. For this there are several reasons. It is not simply the visible product of brains or skill that the world pays for; the world also pays for what man contributes to life. If your personal life is inferior, you give your vocation the stamp of inferiority; and a "common" atmosphere, so detrimental to the progress of any enterprise, goes with you, wherever you may be employed. If you carry an atmosphere of worth, advancement is in store without fail, because the world does recognize worth, and pays well to secure it. It is not only the work, but the life that surrounds that work that counts. It is not only the idea, but the words through which it is expressed that carry conviction. And it is not only the ability of the man, but the way he presents that ability that commands attention from the world.

November 21st

Uriel Buchanan

There is one great law which makes it possible to encourage the higher facilities to gradually unfold the divine nature and to overcome the aimless, drifting tendencies of mind. A certain mood may be recalled in thought by an effort of the will. Hold your thought concentrated in the memory of some beautiful experience. Endeavor to feel that you are under the same influences again. This attitude, held to repeatedly, will give greater ability to control your thoughts and to awaken feelings which will inspire and strengthen the mind. If while sleeping you have had a pleasant dream, when you awake endeavor to recall the details of the dream. By holding your mind in line of correspondence with the original vision, you will pass into the same mental state again, and will go to sleep. Create in your mind a vivid memory of some great emotion or impulse you have felt in the past. This attitude of mind will intensify the corresponding faculties of the brain, and by repetition you will be able to hold your thought permanently in any state desired. The first time you attempt to perform a difficult mechanical act, great effort is required to succeed. The second time the act is performed with greater ease, and by repetition the muscles are trained to respond without any conscious effort. The same law applies to all mental attainment. By the intense desire and persistent effort to hold the mind receptive to a high current of influence, the faculties become more and more responsive. Rigid discipline will accomplish wonderful results in this direction. We must have the ambition which will arouse the will and fire the heart with a determined resolve which will give no rest until we have reached the goal of every desire.

November 22nd

Charles Wesley Kyle

We are free to select the thoughts with which we feed our minds, more free than we are in selecting the foods with which we feed our bodies. This is well, for the character of our thoughts is far more important to our health and happiness than the nature of the foods we eat. Clean thoughts not only make clean minds but they also make clean, healthy bodies. A body ruled by a strong, clean mind is best fortified against all of the current ills of life. Your thoughts build into your body the very substance of which it is composed. Thoughts of envy, malice, hatred and all thoughts that lead to despondency, devitalize the blood and affect the body ruinously. Anger is a positive poison to the blood, while thoughts of kindness, cheerfulness and good-will are powerful tonics, stimulating digestion, and contribute, in the most wonderful way, to the harmonious working of all the vital organs of our bodies. When man comes to realize the power of mastership which he wields over his body he will become more cautious in his thinking than in his handling of sharpened tools. He will send out only thoughts of strength, of health, of harmony and love. When he learns to do this he will find that his bodily intelligence will respond promptly and eagerly, every cell in his whole system taking in the full force and character of his thought and, if he has thought wisely and constructively, he will find his body to be a radiant expression of all that he has commanded it to be. Extreme as these statements may at first glance appear, they will be found upon examination to be the most practical and useful truths of life.

November 23rd

Ernest Holmes

God knows good only, and when we are in line with good He knows us; when we are out of harmony with good, we say, "God has forgotten us." On the one hand we have an Infinite Intelligence which has brought us up to where we are today; and having done all that it can for us now lets us alone to discover our own nature. On the other hand we have the Infinite Law — which is an activity of God — and we can use it for what we will, only with this provision, that, in so far as we use it for the good of all, are we protected.

November 24th

Charles Fillmore

Whoever you are and whatever your immediate need, you can demonstrate the law. If your thoughts are confused, become still and know. Be still and know that you are one with the substance and with the law of its manifestation. Say with conviction: I AM strong, immovable Spirit substance. This will open the door of your mind to an inflow of substance-filled ideas. As they come, use them freely. Do not hesitate or doubt that they will bring results. They are God's ideas given to you in answer to your prayer and in order to supply your needs. They are substance, intelligent, loving, eager to manifest themselves to meet your need. God is the source of a mighty stream of substance, and you are a tributary of that stream, a channel of expression. Blessing the substance increases its flow. If your money supply is low or your purse seems empty, take it in your hands and bless it. See it filled with the living substance ready to become manifest. As you prepare your meals bless the food with the thought of spiritual substance. When you dress, bless your garments and realize that you are being constantly clothed with God's substance. Do not center your thought on yourself, your interests, your gains or losses, but realize the universal nature of substance. The more conscious you become of the presence of the living substance the more it will manifest itself for you and the richer will be the common good of all.

November 25th

Mrs. Evelyn Lowes Wicker

The Human Aura. When energy is impressed with a predominant mental thought, not only does it permeate the body but it is radiated in the atmosphere around you. The aura which you hear spoken of often is the extension of the energies of the body. It is around you at all times. It expresses your character and your personality. The predominant thought of the subconscious mind is radiated in your aura. The aura has the power of attraction or repulsion. In your hours of reflection — when you are thinking things over — if you have charged your mind and directed your thought along uplifting, inspiring courageous lines, your aura becomes charged with that type of thought. If you have used the time in worrying or entertaining thoughts of jealousy, malice or destructive thoughts, your aura is charged with those thoughts, and you have lost the power of attracting good. You attract your own kind. Whenever you draw in your circle someone who is not true to you, you must know that it is a result of your own thoughts. The law of attraction brings you your environment. You are creating your law of attraction and if it brings to you people that you do not like, look back and see when it was that you thought along the line expressed by the person who came into your environment. The law of attraction is one of the great laws of the universe.

November 26th

Prentice Mulford

Daily inflowing of new thought brings new power. To him or her who so daily receives, a fresh force is added, pushing their undertakings farther forward toward success. The silent force of your mind then keeps up its steady pressure on other minds who are consciously or unconsciously cooperating with you. In the higher realms of mind are those who are ever joyous, cheerful, and confident of future success and happiness. They have lived up to the Law, and proven it. With them "faith is swallowed up in victory." They know that by keeping the mind in a certain state, properly controlling their thoughts, there is brought a constant inflowing of happiness and power. Because power and happiness must move together. So must sin, pain, and weakness. They know, also, that their every plan (the Law being followed) must prove a success. Hence, life with them must be a constant succession of victories. Of this their faith or belief is as certain as is ours that fire will burn, or that water will extinguish fire.

November 27th

Shirley Bell Hastings

You are seeking truth. As you find truth, practice that truth; live with that truth; carry that truth into all your experience; carry that truth through all your day; make that truth live with you; live it all. You have an equipment within you with which you can create what you will. You are divine in your nature. Realize that. Think of it! You can create what you will. As part of your equipment you have a mind. And more wonderful still, you have the free use of a universal force to carry on and bring to a complete finish that which the mind pictures, images, thinks, decrees, and lives with. You are by nature and by inheritance a free soul, not bound but free. Withdraw into the chamber of your mind. Close the doors for the time being by closing the eyes, ears, touch, taste, smell. Be relaxed in body. Now think, think, think, think — I AM a creative being. I create by thinking an idea, at the same time knowing that I AM connected with a universal force which carries out to fulfillment the idea I AM thinking. That makes me free for I can think what I wish to think.

November 28th

Orison Swett Marden

Our consciousness is a part of our creative force; that is, it puts the mentality in a position to attract its affinity, that which is like itself. A penury consciousness cannot demonstrate a fortune; a failure consciousness cannot demonstrate success. It would be against the law. If you are steeped in poverty and failure, you have no one to blame but yourself, for you are working against the law. You are holding the poverty consciousness, living in the thought of failure. Perhaps you are wondering why you can't create something that will match your ambition, your longings when all the time you are filling your mind so full of discouragement, so full of black, gloomy, despairing pictures, that your whole life is saturated with the failure consciousness. You feel, perhaps, that something, some invisible force, some cruel fate or destiny is holding you back. Something is holding you back, but it is not fate or destiny; it is your discouraged mental attitude, the unfortunate consciousness that you have been holding for years. While you were trying to build on the material plane, you were neutralizing all your efforts by constantly tearing down on the mental plane. You have been obeying the negative law which destroys and kills blights and blasts, instead of the positive law that produces; that creates, builds, beautifies, develops man's godlike qualities and glorifies his life.

November 29th

Ernest Holmes

The one who desires to heal must stop seeing, reading about, discussing, or listening to conversation about sickness. There is no other way under the sun except as we let go of that which we do not desire, and take that which we wish to have. There is too much of this deceiving ourselves into thinking that we can do two ways at once. We may deceive ourselves and possibly other people, but the law remains the same, a law of mental correspondences, and nothing else. We cannot go beyond our ability to realize the truth; water rises only to its own level.

November 30th

Henry Thomas Hamblin

The inner law of life is love, but it is better for us to think of this as cooperation. To the extent that we think, work, act and feel in correspondence with this law, do we find true happiness, peace, satisfaction and the things which are precious above rubies and which no wealth can buy. We see, then, why we should train ourselves to think thoughts of goodwill, instead of those of hate and resentment; of cooperation instead of selfish acquisitiveness; of service rather than personal gain. It is only thus that we can become brothers of humanity: it is only by becoming brothers of humanity that we can ever enter into correspondence, or a state of at-one-ness, with the internal harmony that is Divine. We live in an orderly universe, for behind the disorder on the surface of life is an internal Divine Order. This Divine Order would find expression externally if every man were to come into harmony with it. But "self" stands in the way. Love, good-will, cooperation, these form the key by which man individually can find entrance to this inner harmony and order; and which by reason of his own entrance he can make it easier for his brother to find entrance also.

December

The Within Creates The Without: Daily Meditations

December 1st

Christian Larson

There is a subconscious side to all the faculties in human nature, and if these were developed, we understand how man could become ideal, even far beyond our present dreams of a new race. It is not well however to give the major portion of our attention to future possibilities. It is what is possible now that we should aim to develop and apply, and present possibilities indicate that improvement along any line, whether it be in working capacity, ability, health, happiness and character can be secured without fail if the subconscious is properly directed. To direct the subconscious along any line, it is only necessary to desire what you want and to make those desires so deep and so persistent that they become positive forces in the subconscious field. When you feel that you want a certain thing, give in to that feeling and also make that feeling positive. Give in to your ambitions in the same manner, and also to every desire that you wish to realize. Let your thought of all those things that you wish to increase in any line get into your system, because whatever gets into your system, the subconscious will proceed to develop, work out and express.

December 2nd

Uriel Buchanan

Throughout the domain of nature we see the evidence of progress. Every manifestation is growing and increasing in refinement and beauty. In the barren rock are elements which will ultimately enter the tree and flower. Back of all visible things is the ceaseless workings of an immeasurable force which moves all things forward. This force causes the rock to crumble that the elements it contains may live in higher forms. It causes the dead leaves to fall, and new ones, full of freshness and beauty, to come forth with each return of spring. It causes the tree to send its roots deep into the soil and to reach out with its branches into the air and sunlight, that it may draw nourishment from the earth and.

the heavens. The vast treasures of coal and oil which man takes from the depths of the earth are the accumulated elements of energy drawn from the sun, ages ago, by the trees and the luxuriant foliage of nature. The stately trees which send up their branches and leaves to sway in the wind are literal conductors of new life and energy coming to the earth in atomic rays from the sun. The leaves are the lungs of the trees, which breathe the new life and absorb the element that is ever working in nature to build the more perfect and beautiful.

December 3rd

Robert Collier

The Fundamental Law of the Universe is that you must integrate or disintegrate. You must grow — or feed others who are growing. There is no standing still. You must speed up your rate of motion until you are attracting to yourself all the unused forces about you, or you must give your own to help build some other man's success. "To him that hath, shall be given." To him that is using his attractive powers, shall be given everything he needs for growth and fruition. "From him that hath not, shall be taken away even that which he hath." The penalty for not using your attractive powers is the loss of them. You are demagnetized. And like a dead magnet surrounded by live ones, you must be content to see everything you have drawn to yourself taken by them, until eventually even you are absorbed by their resistless force.

December 4th

Ernest Holmes

The affirmation is the great weapon of the healer; it is in alignment with the way of the original creative spirit and is the true use of the Word of All Power. We need only to say that our word is the law unto the case and calmly state what we want to be done, and then say and do nothing that contradicts it and wait for the fulfillment of that word. There is a power that operates on what we say, and it is done unto us, and we need have no fear about the results.

December 5th

Orison Swett Marden

Many people seem to think that the imagination, or visualizing faculty, is a sort of appendix to the brain, which it is not a fundamental or necessary part of man, and they have never taken it very seriously. But those of us who have studied mental laws know that it is one of the most important functions of the mind. We are beginning to discover that the power to visualize is a sort of advance courier, making announcement of the things that the Creator has qualified us to bring about. In other words, we are beginning to see that our visions are prophecies of our future; mental picture programs, which we are supposed to carry out, to make concrete realities.

December 6th

Prentice Mulford

"FAITH is the substance of things hoped for." If you keep in your mind an image, or imagination, of yourself in perfect health, and full of strength and activity, you keep the forces working to make you so. You are constructing out of the unseen substance of thought a spiritual self (the healthy self hoped for); and this spiritual self will in time rule the material body, and make it like unto itself. If your stomach is weak, refuse in imagination to see it a weak stomach: see it only a strong stomach. If your lungs are weak, see in your mind's eye your lungs as strong. If your body is weak and sluggish, see yourself in imagination as you were when a boy or girl, when your limbs were full of activity, and you took delight in scrambling over fences and climbing trees. You are then putting out the "substance" of the thing or condition of body "hoped for." As you continue to see yourself thus, the gradual change in your physical condition for the better will increase your faith that this law is a truth. Keep to this thought of yourself as strong, active, and vigorous, week after week, month after month, year after year, and you fix more firmly in mind yourself as free from all disease. It will be a confirmed habit, or, as we say, "second nature," for you so to imagine yourself.

December 7th

Henry Thomas Hamblin

There is psychology being taught today, mostly in books from America, that is hurtful and malicious. It teaches the misuse of mind power by means of suggestion. The mind and will are used to compel others to act as desired by the "operator". For instance, a salesman wants to get an order from a buyer of a certain house. While the latter is considering the matter the salesman uses strong mental suggestion that the buyer should sign the order. Unless the buyer is acquainted with this sort of thing he may be compelled to act against his better judgment. This practice of mental coercion is really criminal, although at present not legally so. It is practiced in a variety of ways, but the one who suffers most is the one who practices the method and not his victims. Nemesis awaits all who misuse their mind powers in this way. We can never work against the laws of life without suffering for it very severely. Such mental malpractice as I have described is in complete opposition to the inner law of cooperation already mentioned; therefore it brings disorder and suffering in its train.

December 8th

James Allen

It is not external things, but our thoughts about them, that bind us or set us free. We forge our own chains, build our own dungeons, take ourselves prisoners; or we loose our bonds, build our own palaces, or roam in freedom through all scenes and events. If I think that my surroundings are powerful to bind me, that thought will keep me bound. If I think that, in my thought and life, I can rise above my surroundings, that thought will liberate me. One should ask of his thoughts, "Are they leading to bondage or deliverance?"

and he should abandon thoughts that bind, and adopt thoughts that set free.

December 9th

Venice J. Bloodworth

The law of the subconscious mind is suggestion. The subconscious mind does not think, reason, balance, judge or reject. It simply accepts all suggestions furnished by the conscious mind; whether they be good or evil, constructive or destructive. Therefore the secret of success is to store your subconscious mind with desire, ambition, courage, determination, enthusiasm and faith in yourself. Add to these indispensable attributes love for your fellow man and faith in the ultimate good of all things. Have faith in your inherent power to achieve; it is faith in yourself that attracts success. If you do not limit your capacities they will have no limit. The Universal Mind sees all, knows all and can do all. We share in this absolute power exactly to the extent of our faith, belief and purpose. Our mental attitude is the magnet that draws to us everything we need to bring our desires into being.

December 10th

George Schubel

Our natural desires are spontaneously and continuously shaping themselves into objects of thought, and these into thought-images which are being impressed, developed and reproduced outwardly all the time. By its action upon mind-substance our desires, or mental images, become concrete, outward realities, visible to the physical eye. That is how ALL THINGS which we are able to see, touch and otherwise outwardly sense in this world have come into outward existence either in a universalized or individualized sense. Heretofore, this formulative process has been largely a haphazard one. Our needs, for the most part subconscious, have simply brought this power into action automatically in a perfectly natural way, with more or less outward success. But now, in mental science, we have begun to study the process by watching its operation within ourselves and others, so that instead of an unregulated process it becomes one which can be regulated and controlled. We have come to know the definite mental mechanical action which is set in motion and the definite chemicalization which takes place; that these can be placed on a basis where they can be intelligently and deliberately controlled so that we are able first to select our desires; secondly to consciously shape these desires into objects of thought, and to establish them as thought-images in our consciousness; and then from this point on we can deliberately exercise this power so that what we desire and see inwardly, can be reproduced outwardly as a part of our outward world of things. We are actually able to SEE inner things into outward existence.

December 11th

Christian Larson

The mind of man is conscious and subconscious, objective and subjective, external and internal. The conscious mind acts, the subconscious reacts; the conscious mind produces the impression, the subconscious produces the expression; the conscious mind determines what is to be done, the subconscious supplies the mental material and the necessary power. The subconscious mind is the great within — an inner mental world from which all things proceed that appear in the being of man. The conscious mind is the mind of action, the subconscious mind is the mind of reaction, but every subconscious reaction is invariably the direct result of a corresponding conscious action. Every conscious action produces an impression upon the subconscious and every subconscious reaction produces an expression in the personality. Everything that is expressed through the personality was first impressed upon the subconscious, and since the conscious mind may impress anything upon the subconscious, any desired expression may be secured, because the subconscious will invariably do what it is directed and impressed to do.

December 12th

Ernest Holmes

Let your soul sing today and the song that comes tomorrow will be all the sweeter, will ring out over the vistas of time with an unmistakable clearness. Here is a soul who knows himself and has found life within himself, who has met God today. No more waiting, no more longing, no more weary roads to travel. He has arrived. The goal is won and peace has come at last today.

December 13th

William Walker Atkinson

The mind has many degrees of pitch, ranging from the highest positive note to the lowest negative note, with many notes in between, varying in pitch according to their respective distance from the positive or negative extreme. When your mind is operating along positive lines you feel strong, buoyant, bright, cheerful, happy, confident and courageous, and are enabled to do your work well, to carry out your intentions, and progress on your roads to Success. You send out strong positive thought, which affects others and causes them to cooperate with you or to follow your lead, according to their own mental keynote. When you are playing on the extreme negative end of the mental keyboard you feel depressed, week, passive, dull, fearful, cowardly. And you find yourself unable to make progress or to succeed. And your effect upon others is practically nil.

December 14th

Joseph Murphy

The subconscious mind is amenable to suggestion and controlled by suggestion. When you still your mind and relax, the thoughts of your conscious mind sink down into the subconscious through a process similar to osmosis, whereby fluids separated by a porous membrane intermingle. As these positive seeds or thoughts sink into the subconscious area, they grow after their kind, and you become poised, serene, and calm.

December 15th

Mrs. Adam H. Dickey

Figures are not things but thoughts; they are mental concepts, and as such they are available to everybody. Sometime it will be realized that not only is this true with regard to figures, but that every so-called material object in the universe is but the counterfeit of some divine idea and not what mortal mind represents it to be. The time will come when mortal mind will abandon its belief that ideas are represented by material objects, and when this time arrives there will be no fear of loss of, or damage to, that which we understand to be an idea and not a thing. We shall then be able to realize what Jesus meant when he said, "Lay not up for yourselves treasures upon earth, where moth and rust doth corrupt, and where thieves break through and steal: but lay up for yourselves treasures [right ideas] in heaven, where neither moth nor rust doth corrupt, and where thieves do not break through nor steal."

December 16th

Charles Wesley Kyle

Man is compelled to work out his own destiny, but not alone, for he has an infallible inner guide, aye, the whole universe is in league to assist him in the construction of his ideals. The enlightened minds of all ages have agreed that, "The proper study of mankind is man" and however searching and profound may have been man's study of the forms of life and of Nature in the past, the ultimate word of all science now affirms that the search for truth has driven all further investigation to look for it in the innermost heart and consciousness of man. In the heart of man are the secrets of God. When man shall come to know himself; to know the relationship which exists between himself and his fellowman, with the universe and with the Infinite, his lesson of life will have been learned. Truly, it has taken man a long, wearisome journey to discover that the Source of Life, the perpetual fountain of health and wealth, of happiness and of peace, for which he has so earnestly and vainly sought in every other place, has all the while lain securely hidden within his own heart. God could do no more for man than He has done. He has made him in His own image; clothed him with His every attribute; endowed him with Life, Love and Intelligence; made him a localized center of His own consciousness; given him faculties and powers which are God-like in their nature and all-masterful, in their creative power. He has made man ruler of himself, and given him dominion over all the earth; over the beasts of the fields, the fowls of the air and the fishes of the sea, and He has placed in the heart of man the magical jewel of thought by which he may trace the successive steps which life has climbed from its first clothing in matter to its highest expression in consciousness, and by this same thought He has enabled him to so refine his body that the grosser particles of it may be transmuted into a still more perfect body, into which pain and suffering may not enter; ruled by a mind that shall know no fear and feel no sorrow, save for other's woes, and this sorrow He has lightened by giving man the power to heal and uplift his fellowman. Now, that man finds himself thus equipped there is nothing for him to do, other than to learn how to develop, educate and train himself for the doing of whatsoever work he may desire to do.

December 17th

Robert Collier

In everything God created, the "Word" or mental image came first then the material form. And that is the way it is with you. Get the right image in your mind, put your faith in it and you can bring it into being. You control your destiny, your fortune, your happiness, to the exact extent to which you can think them out, visualize them, see them as already yours allow no vagrant thought of fear or worry to mar their completion and beauty. The quality of your thought is the measure of your power. "The source and center of all man's creative power," writes Glenn Clark, "the power that above all others lifts him above the level of brute creation and that gives him dominion, is his power of making images, or the power of the imagination." There is a very real law of cause and effect which makes the dream of the dreamer come true. It is the law of visualization and belief — the law that calls into being in this outer world everything that we truly believe to be real in the inner world.

December 18th

Venice J. Bloodworth

Silence is Golden Silence is the key that unlocks the vast resources of the universe. Another very important step toward success is to keep your affairs to yourself. Unless it is necessary to discuss your desires from a business viewpoint, do not talk of what you wish to accomplish. Concentrate on your desires, find your goal, and work towards it, but keep your own counsel. When we tell our ambitions, we waste energy and gain a certain satisfaction in hearing ourselves say what we intend to do. The man who is always telling what he is going to do never does anything. Keep silent about every important matter. Ideas that are locked up in your secret self act as a stimulating urge and intensify your thoughts and action. If you do not talk you MUST act. Silence about your affairs gives you an inward strength and power that carries you on to success. When we want to run a mill by water power we first dam up the river.

December 19th

Jeanie P. Owens

This subject of Thought and its power is so wide that I have only been able to touch very lightly upon one or two points. To those who are interested enough and have leisure to take it up as a study, it will prove a most fascinating as well as profitable subject of research; while those who lack the opportunity for study will do well to ponder the matter in their hearts earnestly and prayerfully. It takes no more time nor ability to think beautiful and pleasant thoughts than to think unbeautiful or unpleasant ones. By a little practice the mind may be trained to the habit of dwelling upon "whatsoever things are lovely," and the improvement in health and happiness, the gain to both body and soul that will undoubtedly follow such a habit, will more than repay any little self-denial that may be necessary at first.

December 20th

Prentice Mulford

Our real self is that which we cannot see, hear or feel with the physical senses — our mind. The body is an instrument it uses. We are then made up entirely of forces we call thoughts. When these thoughts are evil or immature they bring us pain and ill fortune. We can always change them for better thoughts or forces. Earnest steady desire for a new mind (or self) will surely bring the new mind and more successful self. And this will ever be changing through such desire for the newer and ever more successful self. All of us do really "pray without ceasing." We do not mean by prayer any set, formality or form of words. A person who sets his or her mind on the dark side of life, who lives over and over the misfortunes and disappointments of the past, prays for similar misfortunes and disappointments in the future. If YOU will see nothing but ill luck in the future, you are praying for such ill luck and will surely get it. You carry into company not only your body, but what is of far more importance, your thought or mood of mind, and this thought or mood, though you say little or nothing, will create with others an impression for or against you, and as it acts on other minds will bring you results favorable or unfavorable according to its character. What you think is of far more importance than what you say or do. Because your thought never ceases for a moment its action on others or whatever it is placed upon. Whatever you do has been because of a previous long held mood or state of mind before such doing. The thought or mood of mind most profitable in permanent results to you is the desire to do right. This is not sentiment, but science. Because the character of your thought brings to you events, persons and opportunities with as much certainty as the state of the atmosphere brings rain or dry weather. To do right is to bring to yourself the best and most lasting result for happiness. You must prove this for yourself.

December 21st

Ernest Holmes

Because we are limited is no reason why the Universe should have limitation. Our limitation is only our unbelief; life can give us a big thing or a little thing. When it gives us a little thing, it is not limited, any more than life is limited when it makes a grain of sand, because it could just as well have made a planet. But in the great scheme of things all kinds of forms, small and large, are necessary, which, combined, make a complete whole. The power and substance behind everything remain Infinite. Now this life can become to us only through us, and that becoming is the passing of Spirit into expression in our lives through the form of the thought that we give to it. In itself life is never limited; an ant has just as much life as an elephant though smaller in size. The question is not one of size but one of consciousness. We are not limited by actual boundaries, but by false ideas about life and by a failure to recognize that we are dealing with the Infinite.

December 22nd

Uriel Buchanan

Let us learn from nature the lesson of progress. Let us cease to look back, to live over in memory the vanished days. We do not want the narrow life, the false beliefs and the discordant environments of our dead selves. There is a spirit of progressiveness within us which cares relatively little for the past. We welcome new experiences, we invite new joys, knowing that what awaits us will surpass anything we have realized before. Incessant change is the inevitable law of life. There is nothing permanent in the boundless universe. To live at one place, to meet the same people day after day, to follow one pursuit in the same locality and to be bound by an unvarying set of habits at the home and the office or workshop, to repeat the same thoughts, to be haunted continually by the same dismal and cheerless moods, will rob the strongest man of courage and keep his body and mind in abject bondage. To banish sickness and the fear of loss and failure, to dispel the weariness and monotony of existence, turn your thoughts on the bright and beautiful in nature. Behold the falling snowflakes, the moving clouds, the driving rain and the ocean surge. Feast on the beauty of woodland scenes and the sublimity of the mountains. Respond to the silent harmonies of the blue skies, the bright sunshine and fields of waving green. By cultivating a love of nature you will keep in the thought current that will exert a powerful influence for good. You will follow the promptings of the higher self. You will advance to higher realms of power and usefulness. You will work in the right direction and will have knowledge and faith in your capacity to draw things needed and to be successful in all you undertake.

December 23rd

Christian Larson

To secure the best results from the power of thought in its various modes of application, we must understand that there is something back of everything that takes form or action in life, and that it is through this something that the actions of mind should move whenever we use thought or suggestion in any manner whatever. When we are conscious only of the body of our ideas, those ideas convey no power. It is when we become conscious of the soul of those ideas that we have aroused that something within that alone produces results in the mental world. Any thought or suggestion that conveys simply the external form, invariably falls flat. There is nothing to it. It is entirely empty, and produces no impression whatever. But our ideas and suggestions become alive with the fullness of life and power when we also convey the real life or the real soul that is contained within the body of those thoughts. We have, at such times, entered the depths of mental life. We are beginning to act through undercurrents, and we are beginning to draw upon the immensity of that power that exists in the vast interior realms of our own mental world.

December 24th

Shirley Bell Hastings

You create any and every condition in your life by thinking that way. As you continually, persistently, determinedly come back, again and again, to an idea and think it there is a Force which is in and about that takes the idea and brings it forth. It pays to think good ideas; it pays to think healthy ideas; it pays to think happy ideas; it pays to think rich ideas. There is a Force which brings forth all that is involved in the idea. Increase is a principle, a law of action. If you can think increase, if you can ask of the Force for increase, then increase of all you have is created for you because there is a Force which takes the principle of the increase idea and brings it forth. Ideas, many ideas, are continually running through the mind. It must be evident that each person is going outwardly according to the general trend of his thinking. The sad part of it all is that so few seem to comprehend this stupendous fact. Those who do realize it and make the effort to change the trend of thinking by getting in new big leading ideas do gradually change the trend of thinking and so get results on the outer.

December 25th

Helen Wilmans

A belief in good, or the all-prevalent Principle of Life, is the foundation rock of a world's salvation from error, sickness and death. A man is all mind. As such he is a bundle of beliefs. What he believes, that he is. Therefore, his beliefs are his realities, even though they may be based on the untenable premise of the existence of evil; yet they are his realities as long as he lives them and believes them. In order to be strong, healthful, intelligent, vital, beautiful, a man must believe in good and only good; or Life and only Life. As I have often said, the whole Bible hinges on two words — "believe" and "overcome." I am now dealing with the first of these words — "believe." Believe in good — which means life and health — and be saved; "believe a lie and be damned." To believe evil is to believe an error, and believing an error is being damned, because no man (being all mind) can escape the penalty of his beliefs. And he who believes in evil (a lie) takes the consequences of his belief in so-called sin, sickness and death, and is thus damned. To cease believing in error is to cease being damned (whether in this world or any other.)

December 26th

Walter C. Lanyon

"Ye shall decree a thing and it shall come to pass" can only be true of one possessing or ASSUMING the God nature. As long as this manifestation of God seems unusual or miraculous, just so long will it be little in evidence to him. But when man comes to the place where "he makes himself as God" — not A God, but as God: of the same nature and substance — then by this ASSUMPTION the natural flow of God-expression will take place, and he will begin to understand he is "under grace." He will understand and accept the truth of the statement, "Joint heirs with Christ," and Son of the Living God. He will begin to make his ASSUMPTION in the secret place within. He will recognize that, being created of God, he must of necessity partake of the nature of God. His ASSUMPTION of his God nature will have nothing to do with the former idea of wishing and hoping for things to come to pass. Once man is conscious of his true self, his decrees will be surrounded with confidence and abandon. He will not find it unnatural that the Son of the Living God should appropriate the gifts of the Spirit.

December 27th

Mrs. Evelyn Lowes Wicker

Genius. When people think of music — love music, practice music, concentrate upon music, read about the composers — in fact, learn all there is to be known about music — they become connected with the musical thought of the world, and a channel for the musical thought-current. If a person has concentrated upon the masters; such as Beethoven, Hayden, Mozart and many others; he becomes a channel for classics, and if he continues persistently, he will become a genius. There are as many planes of thought as there are ideas. To be a genius means only a vision, a persistent concentration, until you become a channel for the thought-current of the universe. If you persist diligently, keeping your vision before you in your practice, you are a success. Energy is the force that is used. If we send out desire with a weak faith we do not get results. Divided attention always means divided energy, and divided energy means scattered forces. Thought is made possible by the life force that is within you. Never scatter that energy. "This one thing I do and that done well, is the best of rule that I can tell." Keep your ideals, keep your vision and concentrate your energy, knowing that energy has taken on the predominant mental impression and that though energy is going out into the world seeking its own kind through the law of attraction and bringing to you a manifestation of your vision. Man has the power to command the negative force energy to build a perfect body; to build success. Do you wonder that certain splendid teachers claim that we are Gods in the making? There is absolutely no limit to mankind's possibilities when he comes into the right realization of his powers. The only limitation there is, is the limitation that he puts upon himself. The forces are all here waiting for us to use them, waiting for us to become conscious of our powers, and then conscientiously, determinedly put them into use.

December 28th

Emmet Fox

Man being manifestation or expression of God has a limitless destiny before him. His work is to express, in concrete, definite form, the abstract ideas with which God furnishes him, and in order to do this, he must have creative power. If he did not have creative power, he would be merely a machine through which God worked — an automaton. But man is not an automaton; he is an individualized consciousness. God individualizes Himself in an infinite number of distinct focal points of consciousness, each one quite different; and therefore each one is a distinct way of knowing the universe, each a distinct experience. Notice carefully that the word "individual" means undivided. The consciousness of each one is distinct from God and from all others, and yet none are separated. How can this be? How can two things be one, and yet not one and the same? The answer is that in matter, which is finite, they cannot; but in Spirit, which is infinite, they can. With our present limited, three-dimensional consciousness, we cannot see this; but intuitively we can understand it through prayer. If God did not individualize Himself, there would be only one experience; as it is, there are as many universes as there are individuals to form them through thinking.

December 29th

Henry Thomas Hamblin

Man possesses, did he but know it, illimitable Power. This Power is of the Spirit, therefore it is unconquerable. It is not the power of the ordinary life, or finite will, or human mind. It transcends these, because, being spiritual, it is of a higher order than either physical or even mental. This Power lies dormant, and is hidden within man until he is sufficiently evolved and unfolded to be entrusted with its use. Thought is a spiritual power of tremendous potency, but this is not the power of which we speak. By thought, man can either raise himself up and connect himself with the 'Power House' of the Universe, or cut himself off entirely from the Divine Inflow. His thought is his greatest weapon, because, by it he can either draw on the Infinite or sever himself (in consciousness, but not in reality) from his Divine Source. Through the Divine Spark within him, which is really his real Self, man is connected with the Infinite. Divine Life and Power are his, if he realizes that they are his. So long as he is ignorant of his oneness with the Divine Source of all life, he is incapable of appropriating the power that is really his. If, however, he enters into this inner knowledge, he finds himself the possessor of infinite power and unlimited resources.

December 30th

John Seaman Garns

We have found that the first Law of Mind for producing prosperity or any other desired objective is that "Mind acts under its own concept of itself." To which we must now add, "This works only when mind 'believes this concept " And with these we must quickly write a third: "That part of mind which does the believing and at the same time furnishes the creative energies for successful operation of ideas is the subconscious. It is impersonal and highly suggestible, and will accept or believe, and will make to work, whatever conscious mind persistently affirms and imagines. These are tremendously important principles as you will readily see, and just as their wrong use accounts for their past failures and our present poverty, so their right use will assuredly bring, in days to come, a power to create new business, a fresh sense of confidence and ability and unexampled prosperity.

December 31st

Wallace Wattles

As a first step toward getting rich, you must believe these three fundamental statements.

There is a thinking stuff from which all things are made, and which, in its original state, permeates, penetrates, and fills the interspaces of the universe.

A thought in this substance produces the thing that is imaged by the thought.

A person can form things in his thought, and, by impressing his thought upon formless substance, can cause the thing he thinks about to be created.

You must lay aside all other concepts of the universe, and you must dwell upon this until it is fixed in your mind and has become your habitual thought. Read these statements over and over again. Fix every word upon your memory and meditate upon them until you firmly believe what they say. If a doubt comes to you, cast it aside. Do not listen to arguments against this idea. Do not go to churches or lectures where a contrary concept of things is taught or preached. Do not read magazines or books which teach a different idea. If you get mixed up in your understanding, belief, and faith, all your efforts will be in vain. Do not ask why these things are true nor speculate as to how they can be true. Simply take them on trust. The science of getting rich begins with the absolute acceptance of this.

Metaphysical / Law of Attraction Books

David Allen - The Power of I AM (2014), The Power of I AM - Volume 2 (2015) The Power of I AM - Volume 3 (2017)

David Allen - The Creative Power of Thought, Man's Greatest Discovery (2017)

David Allen - The Secrets, Mysteries & Powers of The Subconscious Mind (2017)

David Allen - The Money Bible - The Spiritual Secrets of Attracting Prosperity and Abundance (2017)

David Allen - Your Faith Is Your Fortune, Your Unlimited Power (2018)

The Neville Goddard Collection (All 10 of his books plus 2 Lecture series) (2016)

Neville Goddard - Assumptions Harden Into Facts: The Book (2016)

Neville Goddard - Imagination: The Redemptive Power in Man (2016)

Neville Goddard - The World is At Your Command - The Very Best of Neville Goddard (2017)

Neville Goddard - Imagining Creates Reality - 365 Mystical Daily Quotes (2017)

Neville Goddard's Interpretation of Scripture (2018)

The Definitive Christian D. Larson Collection (6 Volumes, 30 books) (2014)

David Allen - ASKffirmations (2018)

David Allen - The Creative Power of Mind - Daily Meditations For A Better Life (2019)

David Allen - The Within Creates The Without: Daily Meditations: Creating Our Lives By Design (2019)

All books are available online

www.ingramcontent.com/pod-product-compliance
Lightning Source LLC
Chambersburg PA
CBHW020419010526
44118CB00010B/325